SHIFRA STEIN'S
DAY TRIPS®
FROM
HOUSTON

Also by Shifra Stein:

DAY TRIPS: ST. LOUIS
DAY TRIPS: MINNEAPOLIS-ST. PAUL
DAY TRIPS: CINCINNATI
DAY TRIPS: KANSAS CITY
POCKET GUIDE TO KANSAS CITY
DISCOVER KANSAS CITY
THE EDIBLE CITY: A RESTAURANT GUIDE

SHIFRA STEIN'S
DAY TRIPS®
FROM
HOUSTON

Getaways
Less Than Two Hours Away

WRITTEN BY CAROL BARRINGTON
EDITED BY SHIFRA STEIN

The East Woods Press
Charlotte, North Carolina

Library of Congress Cataloging in Publication Data

Barrington, Carol, 1935-
    Day trips from Houston.

    1. Houston Region (Tex.)--Description and travel--
Tours. I. Stein, Shifra. II. Title.
F394.H83B37   1984   917.64'14110463   85-71256
ISBN 0-88742055-9 (pbk.)

Local maps by Kathy Kent
Cover design by Kenn Compton
Typography by RJ Publishing, Charlotte, N.C.
Printed in the United States of America

The East Woods Press
Fast & McMillan Publishers, Inc.
429 East Boulevard
Charlotte, N.C. 28203

CONTENTS

Preface, 9

S   O   U   T   H   E   A   S   T

DAY TRIPS DIRECTORY, 147

For those who love the history
and backroads of Texas

PREFACE

After coping with the race-pace of Houston, a getaway trip literally can be a lifesaver. But where to go with little time and even less money? The answer is to explore what lies just beyond that last subdivision and skyscraper on the city's ever-expanding horizon.

In continental America, Texas and its largest city are the last El Dorado — fertile economic fields for those willing to trust and test their own abilities and take chances. It must be something in the air. The seeds of today's Houston were sown more than 150 years ago by risk-takers like Austin and Crockett, Houston and Travis — and their stories thrive just beyond Houston's doorstep.

But history isn't all. Within a two-hour drive you can canoe a primeval swamp, angle for a free crab dinner, or learn to sail. There are ferries to ride, beaches to comb, and quiet country roads to mosey along on bikes. Ever been to a horse farm or a cane syrup mill? With this book in hand you'll find hundreds of things to do within a short drive home.

Take along a good Texas map. Using it with the Wandering the Backroads sections of this book, you can mix and match portions of adjacent trips to suit your personal interests and available time. Do call ahead, though, if you are planning an important stop. Barrington's Law Number One says that facts tend to change the instant they appear in print.

And one hint: in a decade of exploring the backroads around Houston, I've learned to travel Lone Star-style, stopping to chat as I go — and so should you. Texans are among the world's most friendly folk. They showed me where to see wild ducks wing in on the sunrise in a sea rim marsh and taught me how to seine shrimp from the surf and then cook them in salt water on the beach. A chance comment in Eagle Lake led to the historic treasure that is Egypt Plantation, and all the restaurants listed are local recommendations.

There are new adventures open to you — and if you find something special, please share it with me! Together and in future editions of this book we can make Day Tripping around Houston even more fun.

Carol Barrington

USING THIS BOOK

In most cases, hours were omitted because they are subject to frequent changes. Instead, phone numbers are listed for obtaining up-to-date information.

Restaurant prices are designated as $$$ (Expensive: $15 and over); $$ (Moderate: $5 to $15); $ (Inexpensive: $5 and under).

You will also find the symbol □ to denote that credit cards are accepted.

NORTHWEST

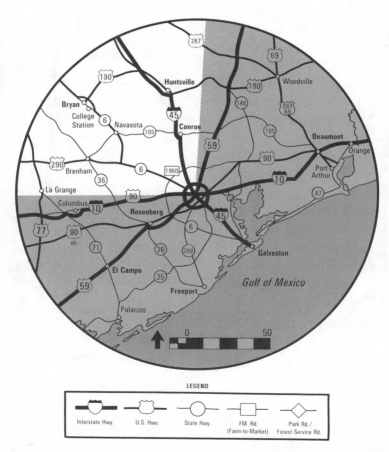

0   50

LEGEND

| Interstate Hwy. | U.S. Hwy. | State Hwy. | FM Rd. (Farm-to-Market) | Park Rd./ Forest Service Rd. |

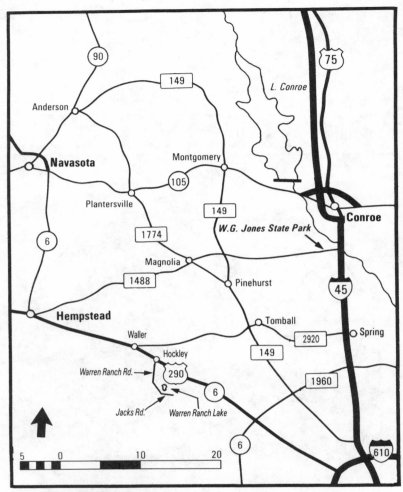

Northwest: Day Trip 1

Day Trip 1

TOMBALL
MAGNOLIA
MONTGOMERY
CONROE
SPRING

TOMBALL

One of the most scenic drives from Houston into the Brazos Valley or
Lake Conroe areas begins by following FM-149 north through rural
woodlands and a series of small towns. Although none of the towns is of
major interest in and of itself, there are several interesting stops along
the way. First up is the farming community of Tomball. Detour east on
Main Street at the FM-149/FM-2920 intersection to enjoy the following
places:

WHERE TO GO

Tomball Community Museum Center. North of Main Street at the end
of Pine Street. Clustered on this cul-de-sac are some bits of the past
collected by the Spring Creek Historical Society. **The Trinity
Evangelical Lutheran Church** was a volunteer construction project of
local German families in 1905, and all furnishings and appointments
today are original to this white clapboard structure. Often used for
private weddings and christenings, it glows again with public services
on Christmas Eve and at sunrise on Easter Sunday. Once each year a
Lutheran service is conducted in both English and German.

    Griffin Memorial House. Next door to the museum center. Built in
1860 by one of Houston's earliest entrepreneurs, Eugene Pillot, it stood
at the intersection of Willow Creek and the Atascosita Trail, the latter
an early stage route in this part of Texas. Sam Houston frequently
spent the night here, waiting for the morning stage, and it also was a
local gathering place and school. The furnishings are Victorian antiques
and constitute, in themselves, the Magdalene Charlton Memorial
Museum.

Pioneer Country Doctor's Office and Farm Museum. Across the way from the Griffin Memorial House is a turn-of-the-century doctor's office where Dr. William Ehrhardt practiced for more than 50 years. The museum contains early farm machinery, tools, etc. The prize exhibit is a 100-year-old cotton gin from nearby Spring. Fee. The Museum Center is usually open Thursday and Sunday, April-September. However, this is a volunteer effort, and the days and hours vary. Best to call in advance: 713-255-2148; 713-351-7222.

WHERE TO EAT

The Hun and the Limey. 601 W. Main, Tomball. The hun is German-born Klaus Schwarzenberger, and the limey is his English wife, Jennifer. Between them, they have created some nifty sandwiches and entrees. This combination pub and restaurant welcomes families and usually has a dart game open to all comers. Open for lunch Monday-Friday, dinner Tuesday-Saturday. $-$$; □. 713-255-2917.

The Viewpoint Restaurant, 29915 Tomball Parkway, (FM 149), Tomball. Country-style food in a casual setting. The chicken-fried steak and salad bar are local favorites, along with the Sunday prime rib special. Cook-owners Ed and Carol Smith make their own muffins and yeast rolls, plus a memorable cabbage and swiss cheese soup. Open daily for lunch and dinner, breakfast too on the weekend. $-$$; □. 713-351-0330.

Renk's El Matador Restaurant, 1231 Alma, Tomball. Son David Renk is El Texano of bullring fame, and bullfighting memorabilia turns this place into a museum. House specials are a strong Tex-Mex menu, a spicy guacamole, and a mighty Margarita. Closed Sunday. $-$$; □. 713-351-7263.

Goodson's Cafe, 27931 Tomball Parkway (FM 149), Tomball. Ma Goodson has hung up her potholders and closed her ramshackle but famous cafe on the outskirts of Tomball. But her recipe for chicken-fried steak as well as some of her kitchen staff continue on at this crisp, new eatery. The menu also offers chicken, burgers, salads, fish for lunch and dinner daily. $-$$; □. 713-351-6490.

MONTGOMERY and MAGNOLIA

From Tomball, drive north on FM-149 to Pinehurst. Those brambles along the railroad tracks are dewberry bushes, loaded in May and just right for picking. If you are so inclined, bring a bucket and gloves and wear stout shoes.

At Pinehurst you must make a choice: either continue straight on FM-1774 to Magnolia and Plantersville or swing to the right, cross the railroad tracks, and follow FM-149 north to Montgomery.

WHERE TO GO

The Texas Renaissance Festival. Six miles north of Magnolia on FM-1774. For six weekends starting Oct. 1, the sights and sounds of Merrie Old England brighten up this 247-acre woodland park. Visitors are encouraged to dress to the 16th-century theme and generally cavort with the jugglers, rope walkers, harpists, minstrels, belly-dancers, and jesters to their hearts content. Fencers joust, Shakespeare struts upon the Globe Theatre stage, and King George and his royal court parade the grounds at high noon. Grand fun for the entire family, with horse and chariot races, assorted craftspersons, and food. Fee. Route 2, Box 650, Plantersville 77363. 713-356-2178 (Houston); 409-894-2525 (Plantersville).

MONTGOMERY

Turning right at Pinehurst and continuing on FM-149 takes you through rolling woodland to Montgomery. An Indian trading post later settled in 1837 by Stephen F. Austin's fourth and last colony, Montgomery prospered for half a century as a major center for mercantile activity in this farming region. Today, Montgomery is a tiny village with a six-block collection of old homes, most of them just north of T-105. In April and December many of the homes are open for public tour. For local information stop in at the Country Store on FM-149, one and a half blocks north of the traffic light or at the Montgomery Chamber of Commerce (409-597-4155) in the community center across from the post office. Allow time for a slow meander through town. There are several antique shops, and the old Methodist churchyard is interesting. Fifteen other sites have historical markers.

WHERE TO EAT

Heritage House, one mile west of FM-149 on T-105. A favorite stop on the Houston-to-College Station run, this antique-filled home is known for its country cooking, chicken-fried steak, and homemade pies and rolls. Open for lunch and dinner Tuesday-Sunday. $$. 409-597-6100.

WANDERING THE BACKROADS

To continue your day trip to Conroe and Spring, travel east on T-105. A turn west on this same highway will connect you with trips 3 through 6 in this sector.

As an alternate to taking T-105 either east or west, continue north on FM-149 through Montgomery to Anderson (Trip 5, this sector). En route, FM-149 crosses a corner of the Sam Houston National Forest and intersects with the popular Lone Star Hiking Trail as well as the faint remains of the Old Telegraph Road. The latter once was the primary route between Montgomery and Houston/Huntsville, carrying wagon trains, stagecoaches, and freight as early as 1843. Today, that old trace is barely discernible in the undergrowth, a slightly less dense path through the national forest.

From Anderson, you can return to Houston via T-90 and T-6.

CONROE

In 1880 the Central and Montgomery Railroad had a line running from Navasota to Montgomery. With the extension of the track in 1885 to a small sawmill run by Isaac Conroe some 15 miles to the east, the town of Conroe came into being. Within five years, Conroe was thriving with 300 citizens and aced Montgomery out of the county seat honor by some 62 votes.

Conroe today needs little introduction to Houstonians, for it is a business and bedroom satellite 39 miles north on I-45. Always the center of a prosperous lumber industry, it hit the financial big time with George Strake's discovery of oil southeast of town in 1931.

Although there is little of history preserved here, it's fun to visit the Creighton Theatre (circa 1930) near the courthouse on North Main. Restored to its vaudevillian grandeur, its stage now holds local performing arts groups. But to day-trippers, Conroe primarily is the gateway to a forest and water playground.

WHERE TO GO

Lake Conroe. Five miles west of town on FM-105. One of the most beautiful lakes in the state, Lake Conroe is 15 miles long and covers 22,000 acres. A complete list of marinas, campgrounds, and public services is available from the Montgomery County Chamber of Commerce, P.O. Drawer 2347, Conroe 77305. 409-756-6644. In addition, there are two excellent private resorts: Walden (713-353-8971; 409-582-6441) and April Sound (713-350-1173; 409-588-1101). Both are open to overnight guests with advance reservations.

W. Goodrich Jones State Forest. Five miles southwest on I-45. Take the FM-1488 turn-off. Logged in 1892 and burned in 1923, this 1,725 acres today is a verdant wildlife refuge under the watchful eye of the Texas Forest Service, part of the Texas A&M system. The Sweet Leaf Nature Trail is self-guided, and a small lake offers picnicking, fishing, and swimming. No admission fee.

Albert Moorhead's Blueberry Farm. Who says you can't grow plump, luscious blueberries in Texas? Mr. Moorhead has ten acres of the high bush variety, and he welcomes guest pickers who call in advance for directions. Bring your own pail. The fee is $1 per pound, and the best picking times are in the early morning or late afternoon from mid-June through July. His farm is deep in the woods between Conroe and Porter, and Mr. Moorhead will meet you and guide you in. 713-572-1265.

From Conroe, your day trip continues south on I-45 to the Spring-Cypress Road exit. Turn left (east) under the freeway to Spring.

SPRING

Back in the late 1800s a community called Spring sprang up to serve the International and Great Northern Railroad as a switching station north of Houston. As the railroads prospered through the turn of the century, so did the town, and in 1902 the Wunche Brothers' saloon was built within a toot of the roundhouse. It had eight rooms upstairs to house railroad personnel.

But we all know what happened to the railroads of America and to many of the small towns that depended on them. By the 1920s the roundhouse had relocated to Houston, and the Texas Rangers had enforced the Prohibition laws by shooting every bottle in the saloon. Then came the depression of the 1930s, and when I-45 bypassed Spring in the 1960s, it was the final blow. The old town area seemed to lapse into a sort of civic limbo as new businesses began to thrive around the new freeway interchange 1 mile west.

So much for yesterday. Today, Old Town Spring is in its second bloom and is a good reason to plan a day trip north of Houston. Specialty shops, antique stores, flea markets, art galleries — all are right at home in the quaint old houses. In general, the shops are open Tuesday-Saturday. If you are coming directly north from Houston, take the 70A exit from I-45 and swing east (right) at the signal on Spring-Cypress Road. When you see the Old Town Spring sign, you're there. Information: 713-353-2317.

WHERE TO GO

Hanna Barbera Land, one-half mile north of exit #68 (Holzwarth Road) from I-45. Family fun with the Smurfs for the 13 and under set, but parents can go on rides too! Closed November-March; open weekends Spring and Fall, daily in summer. Fee. □. 713-526-0914.
Goodyear Blimp Base. 20201 North Freeway. This giant hangar is home to the *America,* and although no public rides on the blimp are available, you are welcome to take a close look.

An attendant explains the Super Skytacular, the computer-controlled night sign that flashes public service messages and Goodyear advertising in glowing lights along the sides of the blimp. Be aware that *America* travels to other parts of the country from early May until late October, and that when she is home, she flies over Harris County six days a week. Monday usually is quiet and a good time to go, but check in advance by calling 713-353-2401. Use the Holzwarth Road exit from I-45.

WHERE TO EAT

Wunche Brothers' Cafe and Saloon. 103 Midway. Back again to its original name after a sojourn as the Spring Cafe, this historic landmark is freshly renovated and offers comfortable lounging outdoors on an upstairs deck or in the patio. Lunch and dinner menus range from steaks and burgers to batter-fried veggies, plus home-baked desserts daily. There's a lively bar also and entertainment on weekends. $-$$; □. 713-350-1902 (the year the place was built!).

The English Lady Restaurant and Tea Room, 431 Gentry. From shepherd's pie to scones and trifle, you'll find the best of traditional English food here, all made fresh on-site. A butler in full livery is your host for the Friday and Saturday night dinners, plus lunch is served Wednesday-Sunday. High teas by reservation only; reservations suggested for dinner. Some art and antiques, plus a small store well-stocked with English biscuits and tinned foods. $$; □. 713-350-9915.

Mary Bell's Tea Room, Preston Street, Old Town Spring. Mary Rehorst and her mother, Bella Salas, combine cooking talents to dish up tasty soups, crepes, salads and sandwiches for lunch Tuesday-Saturday. They bake their own bread, scones, pies, and tarts and post the daily specials on a sidewalk blackboard. $; □. 713-350-2630.

Day Trip 2

HUNTSVILLE
MADISONVILLE
CROCKETT

HUNTSVILLE

In the early 1830s an adventurer and frontiersman named Pleasant Gray thought this rolling, wooded wilderness looked like his former home in Huntsville, Alabama. Because there were good springs nearby, he settled in and established an Indian trading post. By 1836 the tiny settlement of Huntsville was thriving, and in 1847 Sam Houston built his family home and plantation, Woodlands, on the outskirts of town.

Sam's home now seems right downtown, across from the Sam Houston State University campus, and those old Indian trails long since have been formalized into highways. Today, most visitors to Huntsville come via I-45, taking the T-30 turn-off (which becomes 11th St.) and heading east to the center of town.

A fun trail map is available at many businesses and from the chamber of commerce (1327 11th St., P.O. Box 538, Huntsville 77340; 409-295-8113). It will help you find the surviving historic structures around the town square. A motorized trolley, circa 1890s, runs a regular route through downtown on weekdays and during special events on weekends.

WHERE TO GO

Gibbs Bros. Building. 11th and Avenue K (University Ave.). Started in 1841 as a store, the business evolved into the town's first bank because Thomas and Sanford Gibbs owned the only safe. Now this is the oldest business in Texas still on its original site and under the same family ownership.

Henry Opera House. 12th and Avenue K. Such elegance as this must have represented in the 1880s now is hard to visualize. Only the tall windows on the upper floor give a hint to the building's cultural past. Built as a Masonic hall in 1880, it soon became the property of Major John Henry who installed Huntsville's first department store on the

19

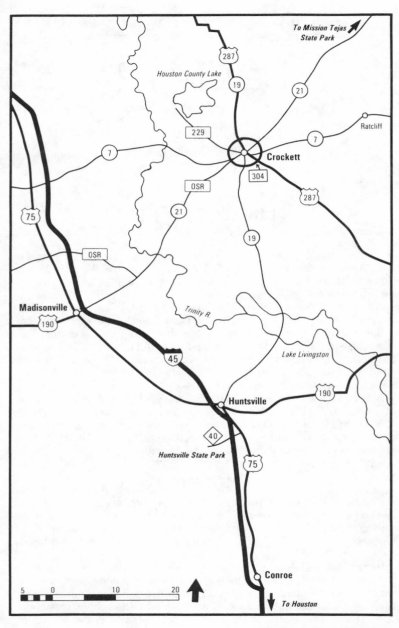

Northwest: Day Trip 2

first floor and converted the second floor into an opera house.

Old Post Office. Between 12th and 13th streets on Avenue K. This turn-of-the-century building is more interesting inside than out, so time your Huntsville trek for mid-day on Thursday when the Junior Service League opens it to serve an inexpensive lunch from 11 a.m. to 2 p.m.

The Walls. Three short blocks east of the town square. This is the original main unit of the Huntsville State Prison. The inmate craft shop is open Wednesday through Sunday, selling crafts made and priced by the prisoners. A walkway to the left of the administration building leads to the arena, site on October Sundays of the roughest rodeo in the state.

Sam Houston State University. Five blocks south of the town square on Sam Houston Avenue (US-75). Founded in 1879 as a normal institute, SHSU had two buildings worth exploring. A disastrous fire in early 1982 destroyed a Gothic wonder known as Old Main (1889) and severely damaged the historic Austin College Building (1853). As a result, the campus has lost much of its character, but it's still nice to stroll.

SHSU Planetarium, Observatory, and Solar Energy Facility. On the campus. From September through May the public is welcome two evenings a month to a special planetarium show, capped by a trip to the observatory and look through the telescopes if the weather is clear. There also are slide and movie presentations. The solar energy facility heats and cools the Physics Building. Free. Call for specific dates. Advance arrangements are appreciated. 409-294-1601.

Sam Houston Memorial Park and Museum. Between 17th and 19th streets on Sam Houston Avenue. During a turbulent life and career that saw him the governor of Tennessee, a general in the Texas Army, the victor at the battle of San Jacinto, and the first president of the Republic of Texas, Sam Houston had many homes. None was as lovely or as beloved by him as Woodlands, built in 1847. Restored in 1981, this square log house with its white clapboard siding is just one of the pleasures in this delightful shady park.

Start at the museum, touring the right wing first to keep the chronology straight, and then visit Woodlands with its separate kitchen, Houston's law office and a blacksmith shop. Close by are the War and Peace House and the unusual Steamboat House where Houston died in 1863. The docents in both homes speak of Houston and his wife Margaret as if they might return at any moment. The small lake shaped like the state of Texas was a fresh, bubbling spring during Houston's time, and today it's a pleasant place for a picnic lunch. Open daily (except major holidays). Free. 409-295-7824. Spring visits get a bonus of flowering dogwood and azaleas. Sam Houston's grave also is interesting, across town at Oakwood Cemetery.

Oakwood Cemetery. Two blocks north of 11th Street on Avenue I. Congratulations, you just drove the shortest official highway in the state. Those two blocks of Avenue I are Texas State Highway One. Houston sleeps with good company at this historic cemetery. Deeded as a free burial place in 1847 by Huntsville's founder, Pleasant Gray,

Oakwood has several tombstones noting burial dates as early as 1834.

Huntsville State Park. Eight miles south of Huntsville. West on Park Road 40 from I-45. This 2,000 + acre park centers on Lake Raven and offers swimming, canoeing, and limited sailing and motor boating. Hiking and birding are excellent, and the forest is dominated by loblolly and shortleaf pine, dogwood, sweet gum, sassafras, and assorted oaks. Good camping and picnicking.

The Gibbs-Powell Home. 11th and Avenue M. This excellent example of Greek Revival architecture was built in 1862 and can be toured by calling 409-291-9500 ext. 17, or 409-295-5767.

WHERE TO EAT

The Junction Restaurant. 2641 11th St. Just look for an 1849 plantation house with an old-fashioned buggy on the front porch. Inside, the house specialties are catfish, fresh seafood, steaks, and chicken. Local legend has it that the skylight (near the salad bar) was built to watch for Indian attacks. $$; □. 409-291-2183.

Conroy's. 1605 Sam Houston Ave. This pleasant lunch room serves light lunches such as salads, sandwiches, crepes, and quiche. $$; □. Open Monday-Friday. 409-295-8716.

The Chef. 1226 17th St. Close to the Sam Houston Museum. This casual place specializes in steaks, seafood, and sandwiches. The owner cuts his own meat, so you get the best. $$; □. Closed on Sunday. 409-291-3357.

King's Candies & Ice Cream, 1112 11th St. on the Square. First cousin to King's Confectionery on The Strand in Galveston, this old-fashioned sweet shop makes traditional shakes, malts, and banana splits at its soda fountain, squeezes lemons for the lemonade, makes its own candy, and serves Blue Bell ice cream. Good place for a lunch sandwich too. Open Monday-Saturday. $; 409-291-6988.

MADISONVILLE

From Huntsville you can follow the old Dallas Highway (US-75) to Madisonville (30 miles) or zoom up I-45. Either way, you roll through pasture lands studded with oaks, cattle, and horses, some of the prettiest country in the state. Madisonville is a quiet town of 3,000 that lost its historic soul in 1969 when its century-old courthouse burned. However, you still can reminisce at several places.

WHERE TO GO

McDermott Quarter Horse Ranch. East frontage road north from the Madisonville turn-off of I-45. One of the more elegant fences in Texas identifies this 2100-acre spread, a breeding and training farm with its own racetrack. Tours can be arranged if you call in advance. No drop-ins please — this is a working spread. Four white pillars mark the entrance drive leading to the ranch office. 409-348-3555 or 348-2768.

Madison County Lake. One-half mile west of I-45 on T-21. This small lake has good bass and perch fishing. Try your luck from the banks during a picnic.

WHERE TO EAT

The Woodbine Hotel. 209 Madison, two blocks north of the town square. This Victorian rambling wonder was rescued from ruin in 1981 by an energetic young Houston couple, Randy and Lynne Parten. Built in 1904, the hotel now has seven guest rooms with private baths and queen-size beds, plus antique furniture. Weekend reservations should be made a couple of weeks in advance. □. 409-348-3591.

If you can't stay overnight, at least drop in at the hotel restaurant and admire the handsomely restored pecan and pine woodwork. The dining room is Victorian casual with linen and fresh flowers on the tables. House specialties include prime rib, steak, and homemade soups and cobblers. Reservations suggested. $-$$; □. Closed Sunday afternoon and Monday. 409-348-3591.

WANDERING THE BACKROADS

The "OSR" turn-off, 10 miles north of Madisonville on I-45, is a meandering country drive with more than a touch of history. While the initials stand for the Old San Antonio Road, it also is known as El Camino Real because it was created by the order of the King of Spain in 1691. The Spaniards, through their control of Mexico, claimed Texas from 1519 to 1821, but the French coveted this rich, wild land also, sending explorers into Texas in the late 1600s. To reinforce its claim, Spain created a series of missions in East Texas and blazed this road to bolster and serve those primitive outposts. Today, OSR follows, after a fashion, T-21 from San Marcos northeast to the Louisiana border, one portion linking the Madisonville area to Crockett.

Turning west on OSR from I-45 takes you through the tiny but historic community of Normangee enroute to Bryan-College Station and Day Trip Three, this sector.

As an alternate to Madisonville, consider a Huntsville-Crockett exploration, slightly outside our two-hour driving limit (117 miles) but rich enough in history to merit consideration.

CROCKETT

Davy Crockett and two companions had to do some fast talking here. Local folks found Crockett's campsite near this area in 1836 (the trio was en route to destiny at the Alamo) and nearly hung them as horse thieves! The fifth-oldest town in Texas, Crockett's history is easy to trace. Visitors should start at the traditional Spanish square in the heart of town and then go exploring. For advance information, contact the Crockett Chamber of Commerce, 700 East Houston, P.O. Box 307, Crockett 75835. Call 409-544-2359.

WHERE TO GO

Monroe-Crook Museum, 709 East Houston Ave. Built in 1854 and noted for its Greek Revival architecture, this historic home is open for public tour on Wednesday morning and weekend afternoons from March to December. Free, but donations are appreciated. 409-544-5280.

Downes-Aldrich Historical Home. 207 North Seventh St. Listed in the National Register of Historic Places, this Victorian survivor now is the Historical and Cultural Activities Center for Crockett. 409-544-2359.

Davy Crockett Spring. West Goliad at the railroad underpass, west of the town square. The spring still flows and serves as a public drinking fountain at what is thought to be Crockett's campsite.

WHERE TO EAT

Butche's Catfish, Shrimp, & Bar-BQ. T-19 south, if you are hungry for these Texas specialties. $. 409-544-5321.

The Royal Restaurant, 112 South Fifth, on the square. House specialty is chicken-fried steak. $-$$; □. 409-544-3863.

Crockett Inn, Loop 304 east. An excellent salad bar and homemade breads complete the steak/fish/chicken menu. Specials debut at lunch and at the Sunday buffet. Open daily for lunch and dinner. $-$$; □. 409-544-5611.

King's Inn. Loop 304 east. The daily buffet features rib-stickin' cowboy country food — a good buy for families and budget-watchers. Closed Sunday. $; □. 409-544-2294.

WANDERING THE BACKROADS

If you feel like extending your drive well beyond the two-hour limit, continue north on OSR (T-21) from Crockett through the Davy Crockett National Forest to the Mission Tejas State Historical Park. The Rice family log home is special here, built between 1828 and 1838 and used as a stage stop. Nearby is a commemorative log structure similar to the old Spanish mission established here in 1690 to serve the Tejas Indians, the first of its kind in Texas.

A second option is to follow T-7 some 20 miles east of Crockett to the Ratcliff Recreation Area, and a third suggestion is FM-229 northwest from Crockett to Houston County Lake. Locally this is considered the best bass fishing lake in the state.

Taking US-287 southeast from Crockett takes you through the Kickapoo Recreation Area near Groveton and hits the northern limit of the Livingston-Woodville day trip in the northeast sector of this book.

Day Trip 3

BRYAN-COLLEGE STATION
AND THE BRAZOS RIVER VALLEY

BRYAN-COLLEGE STATION

From Houston follow T-6 and US-290 north to Hempstead and continue north on T-6 through Navasota into Bryan-College Station.

These joint communities tend to have a single connotation to Houstonians — Texas A&M University. And, while visitors to that sprawling campus find much of interest, there are many other things to do in the vicinity of Aggieland.

Bryan and College Station today flow together into a combined metropolitan area that ranks first in growth in the state and sixth in the entire country, according to the 1980 census. Not bad for a slow starter. This rich sliver of agricultural land bounded by the Brazos River on the west and the Navasota River on the east was sparsely settled until the advent of the Houston & Texas Central Railroad in 1866. The reconstruction years after the Civil War were rough on the young town of Bryan, and it wasn't until the formal opening of Texas A&M College in 1876 that the area settled down to some semblance of respectability.

Some of the footnotes on Bryan's past are interesting. The original street grid inadvertently provided for today's traffic by making Main Street wide enough to turn a five-yoke oxteam, and the college was deliberately sited on the open prairie 5 miles south of town so as to be well removed from the influence of demon rum flowing freely from Bryan's saloons.

An information-loaded historic map covers Bryan's old commercial and residential districts as well as what remains of several small pre-Civil War settlements outside town. This and other area guides are found at the Bryan/College Station Chamber of Commerce Convention & Visitors Bureau, 715 University Dr. East, College Station, Tx. 77840. 409-260-9898. Open Monday-Friday. Write in advance for maps and brochures if you intend to explore on a weekend. Leaving Texas A&M to its own section following, here are some suggestions of what to see in Bryan-College Station.

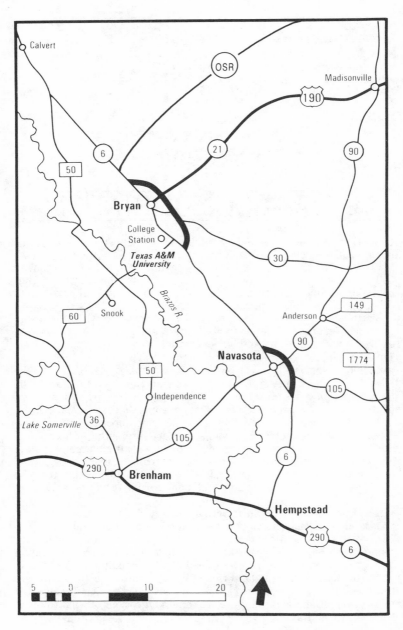

Calvert

OSR

Madisonville

190

6

21

90

50

Bryan

College
Station

*Texas A&M
University*

30

Brazos R.

60

Snook

149

Anderson

1774

Navasota

90

50

105

Independence

Lake Somerville

36

105

6

290

Brenham

Hempstead

290

6

5   0   10   20

Northwest: Day Trip 3

WHERE TO GO

Brazos Center. 3232 Briarcrest. Take the Briarcrest exit east from T-6 bypass. This is the special events place for the area, hosting giant weekend antique shows in March, July, and October. Year-round visitors can enjoy the Brazos Valley Museum of Natural Science and a small nature trail on the grounds. Free. Open Tuesday-Sunday. 409-779-8338 (center); 409-779-2195 (museum).

Texas World Speedway. Six miles south of College Station on T-6. Who needs Daytona or Indianapolis? Everything from Indy and NASCAR cars to 18-wheelers test their race times on this Texas oval, the world's fastest 2-mile track. Advance tickets are available in Houston from Ticketron and Ticketmaster, and racing fans are welcome to camp on the infield. If you like racing, get on the mailing list: P.O. Box AJ, College Station 77840. 409-693-2500.

Canoe Float Trips on the Brazos River. First, so you'll sound like a native, it's pronounced Braa-zas, not Bray-zos as you might expect from the spelling. Generally a quiet and scenic river, the Brazos can be an enjoyable one- or two-day float. Canoe rentals available from Canoes Ltd., 1212 Berkeley, College Station 77840 or by calling 409-693-7307. They will advise on dangerous parts of the river, and put-in and take-out points, but plan on a two-car safari — the rental shops do not provide livery.

If you have your own canoe, you'll find information on the Brazos in several river books available at local bookstores.

Birding. The Brazos Valley is very rewarding with an enormous variety of bird life. A self-guided tour covering five areas and a list of birds common to the Brazos County Arboretum are available from the con-vis bureau previously mentioned. More information and check-list forms can be had from the Brazos Ornithological Society, P.O. Box 9181, College Station 77840.

EXPLORING TEXAS A&M UNIVERSITY

Even if you haven't a prospective student in tow, this handsome 5,142-acre campus has much to offer. Located in the heart of College Station and hard to miss on the west side of T-6, Texas A&M was the first public institution of higher education in the state. Originally an all-male military college, A&M now has a co-ed enrollment in excess of 37,000 and is in the top 20 schools nationally in funding for scientific research.

Aggie traditions are stories in themselves. Ask about the Elephant Walk, the Twelfth Man and Silver Taps at the Visitor Information Center for an insight into what makes Aggies so loyal to their Alma Mater.

Rudder Tower. At University Center on Joe Routt Boulevard. The Information Center in the lobby introduces you to the university through a multi-media show, and campus guides are available, but only if you have a prospective student. Also here: campus maps, an excellent booklet about the school, and admission information. The free visitor's parking lot is adjacent to the building. Open daily. 409-845-5851.

Memorial Student Center, (MSC). Also in the University Center. Visitors enjoy the Buck Schiwetz paintings in the Schiwetz Lounge; the Centennial Wood Carvings in the corridor between the student lounge and the cafeteria, six walnut panels that trace the history of the school from 1876; the Metzger-Sanders Gun Collection in Room 342, antique and historic firearms, as well as the Sam Houston Sanders Commemorative Colt Collection; the Walter and Cordelia Knott Wagon Collection, in the southwest wing of the Forsyth Alumni Center; the Aggie Ring Collection, also in Forsyth Center; and the Texan Campaign Staffordshire China (circa 1850) in the student lounge. Visiting art collections as well as current student work often are exhibited in the gallery near the student lounge.

Oceanography and Meteorology Building. Super view from the 15th floor. The "working collection" library in room 1103 of the Oceanography Department and the specimen room (706) are interesting and open to the public at specified times. Tours by advance reservation only. 409-845-7211.

Nuclear Science Center. Off-campus, near the Easterwood Airport. This multi-million dollar facility houses the largest nuclear reactor on any campus in the southwest and produces radioactive isotopes for scientific research. Tours Monday-Friday. 409-845-7553.

Floral Test Gardens. On Houston Street across from Moore Communications Center. Some 1,000 varieties of seeds and bulbs are grown here annually, part of the all-American seed-testing program across the country. Questions: Department of Horticultural Sciences, 409-845-5341. Picnic areas are nearby.

Tours also can be arranged through the Cyclotron Institute (409-845-1411); Data Processing Center (409-845-4211); Floriculture Greenhouses (409-845-5341); and the Veterinary Medicine College (409-845-5051).

WHERE TO EAT ON THE A&M CAMPUS

Rudder Tower Dining Room. 11th floor panoramic restaurant serving lunch only Monday through Friday. $. There also is a cafeteria in the Student Center. 409-845-1420.

The Creamery. In the Meat Science and Technology Center, adjacent to the Kleberg Building. The best chocolate ice cream in the world is sold here, along with milk, butter, cheese, eggs, and meats grown on the university's farms. Open weekdays.

WHERE TO EAT

Fish Richards Half Century House. 801 Old College Rd., College Station. This is where Aggies bring their parents or special dates. Imaginative food is served in an interesting old house. No solid dress code, but you'll feel conspicuous in jeans. Reservations are suggested.

Take a chance if you're just passing through. $$$; □. Closed Sunday. 409-696-4118.

Black Forest Inn. On the north side of T-30, 20.8 miles east of Bryan-College Station toward Huntsville. Trudie Adams' skill with the classic bourgeois food of Europe as well as our own fresh Gulf seafood brings devotees from as far away as Austin and Dallas, just for a meal. Everything is fresh and made from scratch with no additives or preservatives, including Trudie Adams' own salad dressings and mayonnaise. Should you have to wait for a table, feel free to select a record from the extensive classical music collection or a good book and settle down on a sofa in front of the fireplace. Reservations are almost a necessity, particularly for Sunday brunch or if your party numbers four or more. $$; □. Closed Monday. 409-874-2407.

Farmer's Market and Delicatessen. 2700 Texas Ave. in Bryan. Locally loved for their poor-boys, spaghetti and sweet goods. $. 409-779-6428.

WANDERING THE BACKROADS

From College Station, turn west on FM-60 at the University Drive signal and follow the local folks some 15 miles to Snook (pronounced Snuk). The big attractions, especially on Saturday mornings, are oven-fresh breads, pies and kolaches at the Snook Bakery (409-272-8501) and fresh sausage from Slovacek's (409-272-8625).

As an alternate to returning home from Snook through College Station, backtrack only as far as FM-50 and swing south to Independence and Brenham. Those fine fields you pass north of Independence are part of the Texas A&M Experimental Farms.

If your wanderlust really takes over and you want to stretch beyond the two-hour driving limit, continue north on T-6 30 miles from Bryan-College Station to Calvert. Established in 1868, this nice old town is the unofficial antique center of Texas. There's a flea market the first Saturday of every month, and the Robertson County Pilgrimage opens many of the vintage homes to visitors every April. Calvert's Main Street is a 12-block collection of old brick and iron-front buildings, most of which now house antique shops that are open Thursday through Monday. For information on Calvert, call 409-364-2559.

You can return to Houston one of three ways. The first is the simplest — just reverse the route you followed coming up.

The second is a bit more scenic. Follow T-6 south to Navasota and swing east on T-105 toward Conroe. Turn south on FM-1774 for a forest drive through Plantersville and Magnolia before connecting with FM-149 at Pinehurst. FM-149 south intersects I-45 inside the Houston city limits.

If you feel like exploring more from Bryan-College Station, go east on T-30 to Huntsville (Trip 2, this sector) and then scoot south on I-45 to home.

Day Trip 4

PRAIRIE VIEW
HEMPSTEAD
CHAPPELL HILL

(See map, p. 31)

PRAIRIE VIEW

The primary path from Houston into this northwest sector is US-290, rambling its way through a lot of interesting country en route to Austin and points west. Even small towns like Prairie View and Hempstead have a past. Take a few minutes to explore on your way.

Prairie View today is home to Prairie View State University, but just over a century ago it was the site of the Kirby Plantation, known as Alta Vista. Deeded to the state in 1876 for use as a college for black youths, the old mansion was the school's first educational building. It has vanished now, along with de facto segregation, but look for St. Francis Episcopal Church, a small frame building (1870) moved to the campus from Hempstead in 1958. The first Episcopal church north of Houston, it still has the original pews, handmade by the first congregation.

WHERE TO GO

Boy's Country. Thirty miles northwest of Houston on US-290, then right 2 miles on Roberts Road. On the way to Prairie View you can visit this working ranch which provides a stable home environment for 120 boys. During the spring and summer the ranch's small but neat nursery sells hanging baskets, herbs, and perennials at excellent prices. 713-351-4976.

Spring Creek Parachute Ranch. Approximately 11 miles northwest of Houston via US-290 to Hockley. One Saturday's course of instruction will have you into your first jump, weather permitting. Equipment is included, and no reservations are necessary. Open weekends, year-round. 19815 Becker Road, Hockley 77447. 713-351-0194.

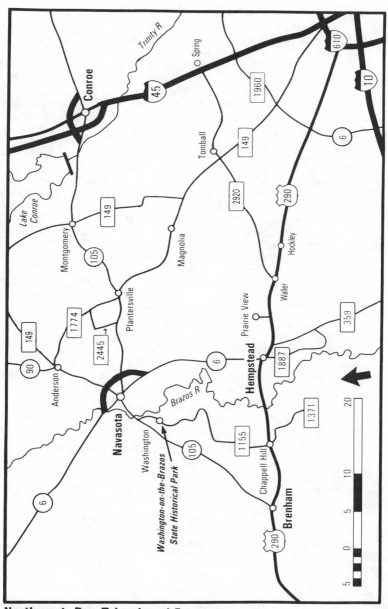

Northwest: Day Trips 4 and 5

Ultra Light Flight Park. Thirty miles northwest of Houston on US-290, then right on Roberts Road at Boy's Country sign; left on Zube Road. A triple fun possibility. In addition to sales, service, rentals, and lessons for ultra-light airplanes, this entrepreneur offers BMX Motocross for motorcycle enthusiasts, and Rent-A-Row farming. For a low all-season price you can rent 100 foot, irrigated rows of farmland and grow your own produce. 713-373-3055.

Birdwatching at Warren Ranch Lake. Two miles west of Hockley on the left side of Warren Ranch Road. As you pass through the tiny community of Hockley en route to Prairie View, Hempstead, and points beyond, turn left at the tallest rice dryer for a special nature experience. The largest winter concentration of ducks and geese in North America is found in the rice fields of this area, and the 50 wild acres of Warren Ranch Lake have been known to host as many as 20,000 ducks and geese at one time. The lake itself is private and protected, but the viewing is great (with binoculars) from the shoulder of the road. With luck, you'll also spot some Bald Eagles — an endangered species and America's national bird. For information, call the Houston Audubon Society, 713-932-1392.

Bar C Ranch. Turn south on Becker Street, 6.5 miles west of Cypress on US 290. Owned by Aubrey and Laverne Chudleigh, this 1200-acre working ranch is a good look at what rural life is all about and how food is grown. Mr. Chudleigh gives a tour of the fields, explaining the different crops and how they are grown, plus you can feed the farm animals, pitch horseshoes, or even swing from a rope into a pile of hay. Open Monday-Saturday by advance arrangement only. Fee. Information: 15011 House, Hockley 77447. 713-373-1078.

HEMPSTEAD

It's hard to believe that this quiet town once was known as Six-shooter Junction and that for several decades after the Civil War it was a wild and woolly place. The rolling country south of Hempstead was settled as early as 1821, although only scattered historical markers tell the stories now.

Hempstead was platted in 1856-57 as the terminus for the Houston and Texas Central Railroad, an early line that tooted over much of Waller County before expanding north to Bryan-College Station. During the Civil War the railroad made Hempstead a major supply and troop depot for Confederate forces, and when the war ended, the defeated men began their long walks home from here.

Hempstead literally was the turning point in Texas' battle for independence from Mexico. Sam Houston and his retreating forces camped and re-grouped here from March 31 to April 14, 1836, and then began their aggressive march to San Jacinto and their ultimate victory over Santa Anna and his Mexican army. A brief jaunt down FM-1887 today finds a historical marker about the Texian Army camp.

Hempstead slowly is re-awakening to its heritage, but at present most of the old structures remain in private hands and are closed to the public. A windshield tour of the quiet residential streets on either side of US-290 has rewards such as Coburn Cottage, 327 12th St.; the Ahrenbeck-Urban Home, 1203 Bellville Highway; and the Houx House, on the corner of US-290 (also called T-6 locally) and New Orleans.

One good reason to stop in Hempstead en route to Washington County is Dilorio's thriving produce market on US-290 at the southeastern edge of town. There is adequate off-street parking, but re-entering US-290 remains hazardous.

WHERE TO EAT

The Hempstead Inn. 435 10th St. (US-290/T-6). This old railroad hotel was built in 1901, 100 yards closer to the tracks than its present site. It closed in 1968, only to rise to useful life again in 1981 under the talented hands of Ann and Ghazi Issa. Restored with love, new plumbing, electricity, roof, and the stylish trimmings it might have had in 1901, the hotel again serves lunch and dinner, boarding-house style. Ghazi is a Cordon Bleu-trained chef, and the specialties include fresh vegetables, homemade breads, two meat entrees at lunch, and three at dinner. Guests help themselves to what they want from never-empty bowls on the table, so you can sample it all if you wish. $$. Closed Monday. 409-826-6379.

Dairy Palace. 240 Austin St. (On US-290/T-6). It's bright and clean, and you'll find the best of Blue Bell ice cream here, along with sandwiches, burritos, hamburgers, and tacos. 409-826-2428.

CHAPPELL HILL

From Hempstead, follow US-290 north and west 11 miles to the intersection of FM-1155 and jog north to your next stop, Chappell Hill.

This charming village just north of US-290 may be the Brigadoon of Texas, so true is it to its time. Settled in 1847, Chappell Hill thrived as a stage stop on the Houston to Austin/Waco run and became the cultural center of Washington County, home of two four-year universities. But the fickle tides of progress soon moved on, and visitors today often feel they have stumbled on a quiet place left over from the 1880s.

The universities are long closed, their charters transferred to become the seeds of Southwestern University in Georgetown, Southern Methodist University in Dallas, and the University of Texas Medical Branch in Galveston. But the old Stagecoach Inn still is here, a private home restored in all its antique glory, and the Farmer's State Bank, circa 1900, has its original brass teller's cage and was the last bank in the region to register its customers by name instead of magnetic codes and computers.

There's a latch-key library — local folks all have their own keys — and more than 25 historical medallions are scattered through the settlement.

Buy an ice cream cone at the old drug store and then take a nostalgic walk through Lesser's Grocery, stocked with kerosene, seed spuds, and local sausage just as it was in great-grandfather's day.

A section of Main Street and seven other local sites have been added to the National Register of Historic Places.

Chappell Hill Historical Museum and Methodist Church. On Church Street, one long block east of Main. The museum is in an old school and is staffed Sunday afternoons only. The church has stained-glass windows and is open for Sunday services. A donation is appreciated.

Rock Store Museum. East side of Main Street near the bank. The prime display is the town's history, embroidered and appliqued on two 30-foot-long cloth panels. Open weekend afternoons or when the local ladies feel like socializing. Donations are appreciated. Special appointments: 409-836-5883.

Stagecoach Inn. Main and Chestnut streets. This is the best look at the past in all of Washington County. Listed in the National Register of Historic Places, this beautiful Greek Revival structure was built in 1850 and was a busy stage stop through the Civil War. Note the Lone Star and 1851 date inscribed on the downspout heads, the detail of the Greek-key frieze on the cornice encircling the house, and the old-fashioned flower gardens. Sorry, no overnight guests, but guided tours for four or more can be arranged in advance. Fee. Call 409-836-9515. Through this number you also can arrange tours of other historic homes in the Chappell Hill area. Also, there is an antique shop open to the public in the historic Weems house behind the Stagecoach Inn.

Elizabeth and Harvin Moore, owners of the Stagecoach Inn, also operate Lottie's B&B, a 2-bedroom cottage across Main Street from the inn. Named for Charlotte Hargrove, the Stagecoach Inn proprietor from 1851-58, Lottie's is a Greek Revival cottage from the 1850-70 period and furnished in antiques. The nightly rate includes continental breakfast fixings in the kitchen and use of the entire cottage.

Waverly. One-half mile east of Main Street on Chestnut Street (FM-2447). Watch for a one-story white plantation house with columns. This 1850s Greek Revival treasure is special for its original foundation, wood siding, kitchen, and beveled-glass front doors. The Waverly Shop sells antiques in the old kitchen, and tours of the house can be reserved in advance. Fee. 409-836-5067.

Browning Plantation House. One mile south of US-290, off FM-1371. Restored and listed in the National Register of Historic

Places, this three-story wood home was built in 1856 and is graced with porches front and back. Groups of four or more may arrange tours through Mrs. Harvin Moore at the Stagecoach Inn. Fee. 409-836-9515.

Tours of all the historic homes also can be arranged by writing Historic Homes of Chappell Hill, Drawer E, Chappell Hill, Tx. 77426.

Winkelmann. Four miles east of Brenham on US-290. More than two dozen buildings from Texas' frontier past have been gathered here and now house antique shops, boutiques, a saloon, general store, and an outstanding restaurant. Most of the buildings have been rescued from decay and disuse; the general store once stood in Plantersville, and the dance hall was the Armstrong School building in Sauney Stand, a small community south of Chappell Hill. Special weekend events include gunfighters' competitions, blue grass jam sessions, chili and barbecue cook-offs, etc., and although most are free, there may be a small charge for parking. Open daily, except many of the shops close on Monday and have limited operations January-March. 409-836-3440.

WHERE TO EAT

Bluebonnet Hills Inn. On the westbound side of US-290, between Chappell Hill and Brenham. Good home cooking here, courtesy of former Astro Roger Metzger and his extended family. The menu usually offers a choice of six meats in a dinner that starts with homemade vegetable soup. Roger cooks a catfish special on Thursday nights. Reservations suggested for Friday and Saturday evenings. Closed Monday and Tuesday. $$; □. 409-836-4642.

Cedar Hall Restaurant. An authentic 1850s plantation house at Winkelmann serves up some memorable meals. Open Tuesday-Sunday for lunch and dinner. $$; □. Reservations suggested. 409-836-4991.

WANDERING THE BACKROADS

From Chappell Hill, you can retrace your steps home to Houston via US-290 east — things do look different when you are going the other way — or you can connect with Trip 5 in this sector by taking FM-1155 north just as the early settlers did to Washington-on-the-Brazos. If you prefer to explore around Brenham, return to US-290 and continue west 9 miles to Trip 6, this sector.

Day Trip 5

WASHINGTON-ON-THE-BRAZOS
NAVASOTA
ANDERSON

(See map, p. 31)

WASHINGTON-ON-THE-BRAZOS

From Houston, follow US-290 northwest through Hempstead to Chappell Hill. Continue on FM-1155 north to Washington-on-the-Brazos.

This portion of Texas was crossed by countless trails that were the interstate highways of the 17th and 18th centuries, and numerous highway markers today comment on three major routes. The Old San Antonio Road ran to the Louisiana border and passed to the north of Bryan-College Station. The Coushatta Trail through Grimes County to the north was part of the Contraband Trace, used for smuggling goods from Louisiana into Spanish Texas. A third trail, La Bahia, went from Goliad to the lower Louisiana border, sometimes running in tandem with the Old San Antonio Road.

In 1821, one of Stephen F. Austin's first settlers started a small farm and ferry service where the busy La Bahia Trail forded the Brazos River. In 1835 the settlement was capitalized as the Washington Town Company, lots were auctioned, and the raw beginnings of an organized town began to emerge on the river bank.

March of 1836 was a fateful month for Texas. While Santa Anna was devastating the Alamo, some 59 men were creating the Republic of Texas at a constitutional convention at Washington-on-the-Brazos. (Contrary to current popular opinion, those delegates did not choose the armadillo as the official mascot.)

Washington later served twice as the capital of Texas, but ultimately lost that honor to Austin. By-passed by the railroads, the community literally disappeared after the Civil War.

WHERE TO GO

Washington-on-the-Brazos State Historical Park. Today, only a handful of relatively new wood buildings and the park's special structures mark where Texas began. Road signs clearly mark the route to the park headquarters. All of the following are within the park boundaries and charge no admission fee.

Independence Hall. Site of the signing of the Texas Declaration of Independence, this simple frame building is reconstructed on the original site. An audio-visual program comments on the 1836 convention.

Star of the Republic Museum. Start with the slide presentation for a good historical perspective, and then take the self-guided tour through a variety of exhibits that include a rare 1845 mail coach from Galveston. The museum also attracts excellent traveling exhibits and is noted for its reference collection of Texana material, including old maps, documents, letters, and rare books. Guided tours can be reserved in advance.

Barrington. This was home to Anson Jones, the fourth and last president of the Texas Republic. Furnishings are from that period.

All of the above are open daily, March-Labor Day. Closed Monday and Tuesday, September-February. P.O. Box 317, Washington 77880. 409-878-2461.

Antique Co-op. Everything from dolls and good Texas primitives to Reba's general junk, housed in the old schoolhouse behind the post office. Reba also sells dewberry jelly, fig preserves and wild grape jam, the tastiest in the county. Open Friday-Sunday, year-round. 409-878-2112.

WHERE TO EAT

Old Washington Inn. Nine miles north of Chappell Hill and nine miles south of Washington on FM-1155. Retired Houstonians Emily and Loren Urban have created a jewel of a restaurant worth the drive from Houston in itself. House specialties are an authentic Louisiana gumbo, fresh seafood and homemade pies, cakes, and breads. Beer and wine can be served on the back porch overlooking the pond, and local handcrafts are sold. Open Wednesday and Thursday for dinner; Friday-Sunday for lunch and dinner (reservations required). $-$$; ☐. Route 1, Box 514, Washington 77880. 409-836-1134.

D & K General Store. Two miles northwest of Washington and nine miles west of Navasota on T-105. Local folks claim this has the best and freshest salad bar for miles around. Steaks, hamburgers, catfish, and shrimp are good bets too. Open for lunch and dinner Thursday-Saturday, lunch on Sunday. $-$$; ☐. 409-878-2273.

WANDERING THE BACKROADS

After exploring Washington-on-the-Brazos, continue this day trip by following FM-1155 and T-105 north to Navasota. If you prefer, you can turn south on T-105 to Brenham (Trip 6, this sector) or follow FM-1155 south to Chappell Hill (Trip 4, this sector).

NAVASOTA

Settlers responding to Stephen F. Austin's ads for colonists founded this town in the 1820s. A generation later, cotton was king of the plantation economy, thriving here on the rich bottom land of the Brazos River.

The coming of the railroad in the 1850s brought even larger profits, and the wealthy farmers splurged on lavish town homes, many of which survive today. Some line Washington Avenue (T-105) as it flows through Navasota, and others require short detours onto Johnson, Holland, and Brewer streets. All are private homes, open only during Navasota Nostalgia Days the first weekend of May. The newly opened Castle Inn at 1403 E. Washington offers outstanding bed and breakfast in an 1893 Victorian mansion. 409-825-8051.

Not too surprisingly, Navasota stood heart and soul with the South during the Civil War, but unpaid Confederate soldiers angrily burned much of the town in 1865. A yellow fever epidemic two years later dealt the final economic blow. Today, this quiet community of 5,000 snoozes in the heart of horse farm country, its grand past only a memory.

Even fewer traces of the area's Indian and Mexican history survive, and visitors are often startled to find a statue of French explorer La Salle in the center of the main road. It memorializes his death nearby in 1687 at the hands of his own men.

Today's explorers of Navasota find a quiet town full of handsome old homes and a few antique shops, those mostly south of the railroad tracks along Washington Avenue. Information as well as walking and driving tour brochures are available from the Grimes County Chamber of Commerce, 117 S. LaSalle (P.O. Box 530), Navasota 77868. 409-825-6600.

WHERE TO GO

Schumacher Oil Mill. Two blocks north of Washington on North LaSalle. Built in 1866 along the banks of Cedar Creek, this cottonseed oil mill was the oldest in the world when it closed to the public, it is interesting just to drive around the massive old building and read the historical marker.

Bank of Navasota. 109 W. Washington Ave. This 1880s building has been restored to its original look and use. Open Monday-Friday, 9 a.m.-3 p.m., Saturday, 9 a.m. to Noon.

Navasota Livestock Auction Co. Three miles east of Navasota on Highway 90. Ranchers from Grimes, Washington, and Brazos counties bring their livestock here for sale. Visitors are welcome to watch the action, but don't scratch your nose or tug on your hat — you may go home with a live calf as a souvenir. Saturday mornings only. Free. 409-825-6545.

The Peaceable Kingdom. From Navasota take T-105 south approximately 8 miles (just past the turn-off to Washington). Turn right on Washington County Road 96, also known as the Old River Road, and take the first right turn. Take this dirt and gravel road 1.7 miles to a yellow cattle guard on the left, and you are at the Peaceable Kingdom.

This residential craft community emphasizes holistic health and uses the whole environment as a teaching tool. Depending upon who is in residence and the time of year, you may see classes on anything from natural dyeing and massage therapy to cultivated and native herbs. Founded by Libbie Winston in 1970, this small farm also has animals, organic gardens, a solar greenhouse, assorted workshops, and a small shop selling live and dried herbs. The public is welcome to visit, and there is some overnight camping (fee), although the accommodations verge on the primitive. Open Wednesday-Sunday. For information on camping or their spring/fall seminar and classes, contact Box 313, Washington 77880. 409-878-2353.

Inspiration House. This retreat for writers is housed in an elegant old Victorian house and offers seminars and meet-the-author sessions every four to six weeks. If you've always wanted to write, this is a good place to start. The seminars are open to the public with advance reservations. 409-825-7005.

Fairweather Farms. T-105 east from Navasota toward Conroe. This beautiful horse-breeding ranch welcomes visitors with advance appointments, particularly August through January. February through July is the busy breeding season, and they may not be able to spare the time to show guests around. No drop-ins please, any time of year. Free. 409-825-7272.

WHERE TO EAT

Ruthie's Cafe. 905 W. Washington. This barbeque place is a Texas classic — six kinds of meat pit-smoked over oak and mesquite. Closed Wednesday. $-$$; □. 409-825-2700.

From Navasota, this day trip continues to the tiny town of Anderson, 10 miles northeast via T-90.

ANDERSON

Time stopped here about 1932, and the entire town looks like a stage set for a Bonnie and Clyde movie. Fact is, one member of the Barrow gang was tried here in the old courthouse, a tidbit duly noted on the building's historical medallion. But Anderson's history reaches back much further than the 1930s.

Established in 1834 as a stage stop on the La Bahia Trail, the town became an important assembly point and arms depot during the Civil War. Those days of glory live again during the Anderson Trek each spring when local folks don period costumes and open their homes to visitors. Best of show is the horse-drawn vehicle parade down Main Street.

The entire town — everything you can see from the top of the courthouse — is listed in the National Register of Historic Places.

WHERE TO GO

Grimes County Courthouse. Top of Main Street. Built of hand-molded brick with native limestone trim, this oldy has its original vault. Note the handsome pressed-tin ceilings with rounded cove moldings in the main hall. Open Monday-Friday.

Oberkampf Drug Store. Cater-corner from the courthouse. Founded about 1850 some 60 feet from its present site, this building dates from 1910, and the drugstore looks as it did at that time. Call the county clerk's office, 409-873-2662, for hours of operation.

Fanthorpe Inn. Bottom of Main Street on the left. One of the state's first stage stops, this old inn was built in 1834 and led to Anderson's being, for a time, the fourth largest town in Texas. Now closed and posted, the inn currently is under restoration by the Texas Parks and Wildlife Commission.

Steinhagen Log Cabin. South of the intersection of FM-1774 and T-90. Built in 1852 by slaves, the walls are notable because they are unspliced hand-hewed timbers. Furnishings are to its primitive period, and tours can be arranged in advance by calling Historic Anderson, Inc., 409-873-2662.

New York Row. Parallels Main Street one block east. This lane is where the town swells lived during Anderson's heyday.

Baptist Church. Left side of Main Street, two blocks south of FM-1774. Built of native rock by slaves in 1855 and still used for services. LBJ's granddaddy once was Anderson's preacher.

WHERE TO EAT

Southern Breeze Plantation. From T-105, turn north on FM-2445 for 3.8 miles. This recently built copy of Andrew Jackson's Hermitage is one of the more innovative restaurants in the greater Houston area. Although the Tuesday-Saturday meal sittings are for pre-reserved groups of eight or more, the "Sampler" luncheon and program one Saturday each month accepts individual reservations.

Only fresh food is used, cooked from scratch and served with homemade yeast breads produced on-site by the Brazos Bottom Bakers. The house is filled with antiques, many of which are for sale, and the grounds are open for rambling. The Sampler luncheon programs are innovative and worth the trip to this north country in themselves.

Recent subjects include "When a Second-hand Woman Takes a Retread Man (or How to Have a Geriatric Honeymoon)" and "A Matinee at the Breeze Bijou." Other Samplers have included hot air balloon rides, a blues singer and guitarist, and such edible delights as baked breasts of chicken with apple and almond stuffing. This wonderful place is run by three zany sisters who also grow and sell fresh bean and alfalfa sprouts, and the baked goods can be bought to take home. $$$. Reservations required. Route 2, Box 3520, Navasota 77868. 409-894-2435.

WANDERING THE BACKROADS

For Houstonians who like country drives, getting home from Anderson via FM-1774 south is pure pleasure. While spring is prime because of the wildflowers, the fall season drive recalls the rolling back hills of Massachusetts. The oaks turn color with the first frost, and Anderson's lone church steeple pokes up through the landscape like a sentinel on a hill.

Day Trip 6

BRENHAM
DIME BOX
SOMERVILLE
INDEPENDENCE

BRENHAM

If it wasn't a 72-mile commute on US-290 each way, Brenham would be overrun with refugees from Houston. This thriving community of slightly more than 12,000 is close to the ideal American small town — old enough to be interesting but new enough to keep up with the times.

Shaded residential streets still sport a number of ante-bellum and Victorian homes, and many of the turn-of-the-century buildings downtown are spiffed up and in use. Just blocks away, it's open country again — thousands of acres of beautiful farmland. In the spring the bluebonnets and other wildflowers are magnificent, a carpet of color rolling to all horizons.

Founded in 1844 and settled by German immigrants during the ensuing two decades, Brenham was occupied and partially burned by Federal troops during the Civil War. Most of the town's surviving history can be seen on a windshield tour, courtesy of a free map and visitor's guide available from the Washington County Chamber of Commerce, 314 South Austin, Brenham 77833. 409-836-3695. Ask here also for guided tours of the downtown historic district.

WHERE TO GO

Giddings-Stone Mansion. Near South Market and Stone streets. This 12-room Greek Revival home was built in 1869 on a hill in what was then country south of town. Now owned by the local Heritage Society, it is being restored and is considered by historical architects to be one of the ten most significant old homes in Texas. You may walk the grounds, but not enter the house at this time.

Ross-Carroll-Bennett House. 515 Main St. This private residence typifies the fanciful fretwork of the Victorian era (circa 1893). What looks like blocks of stone on the exterior actually is cypress in disguise. This is privately owned; please do not trespass.

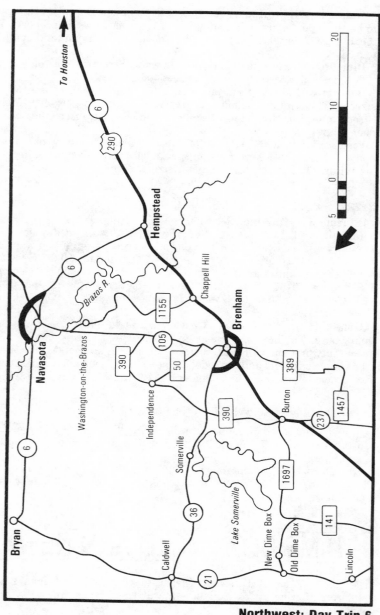

Northwest: Day Trip 6

Giddings-Wilkin House. 805 Crockett. Built in 1843, this is thought to be the oldest house still standing in Brenham. Now the property of the Heritage Society, it sometimes is open as a museum and can be toured by appointment. 409-836-3695.

Blue Bell Creameries. Loop 577 (Horton Street). Free tours and tastes, but call ahead to confirm space. 409-836-7977.

Bassett & Bassett Banking House. Corner of Market and Main streets. This vintage building is freshly restored as part of a Main Street revival in Brenham. Check with the chamber of commerce for open hours.

Fireman's Park. 900 block of North Park. The very old, fully operational carousel here runs on special occasions, such as Maifest.

Savitall. Commerce and Baylor streets. This old grocery store remains in operation and is worth a look.

WHERE TO EAT

Bluebonnet Hills Inn. See Chappell Hill listing, Trip 4, this sector.

Charlie and Lee's. 2107 South Market St. A good place for hamburgers, sandwiches, and soup. They'll fix all to go if you want to picnic in the park or at Lake Somerville. $. Open daily. 409-836-0312.

Ice Cream and Candy Shoppe. Four Corners Shopping Center, US-290 and T-36. This place features ice cream from the Blue Bell Creameries, one of Brenham's claims to fame. $. Open daily. 409-836-5301.

Oma's Haus. 106 S. St. Charles St., two blocks east of the courthouse. The best of German food is featured at this simple cafe, from bratwurst and a delicate schnitzel to blintzes and potato pancakes. The cheese cake and apple strudel are homemade and memorable. Open for lunch Monday-Friday, dinner on Friday-Saturday. $-$$; □. 409-836-0645.

WANDERING THE BACKROADS

After you've toured Brenham, continue your trip via US-290 west to Burton and FM-1697 and FM-141 to Dime Box and some areas of Lake Somerville.

An alternate day trip follows T-105 northeast from Brenham to Navasota (Trip 5, this sector), or you can jog south on FM-389 to Trips 4 and 5 in the west sector.

DIME BOX — OLD AND NEW

The name alone of these two separate communities brings some explorers. Perhaps this explanation will save some time, gas, and tempers.

Old Dime Box is on T-21, sort of around the corner a few miles from New Dime Box on FM-141. Of visitor interest in either place are the historical plaques that explain that the town name comes from the old custom of leaving dimes in the community mailbox on the Old San Antonio Road (T-21) in return for items brought from Giddings.

If you do explore in and around Dime Box, you can get back on your original day trip route by following T-21 northeast to Caldwell and then T-36 south to Somerville. Continuing on T-21 northeast from Caldwell brings you to College Station, Trip 3 in this sector.

SOMERVILLE

Who would think that three little creeks could combine to form a 24,000-acre lake? Dammed in the early 1960s as a flood control and water conservation project, Lake Somerville has become a favorite water playground 88 miles northwest of Houston on T-36.

The town itself serves only as a gas and grocery supply depot — the lake is the big attraction. Popular with boaters, there are seven campgrounds around the lake, two of which are state parks (see listings in back of book). Fishing is good for largemouth and white bass, white crappie, and channel catfish.

The wild birds are varied enough to warrant a folder and field checklist, available free from the Texas Parks and Wildlife Department, Resource Management Section, 4200 Smith School Rd., Austin 78744.

Your day trip continues south on T-36 from Somerville to FM-390. Turn northeast (left) to Independence.

INDEPENDENCE

As far as Washington County is concerned, Independence is where it all started. Originally called Coles' Settlement for its first pioneer, John P. Coles, the town's name was changed in 1836 to celebrate Texas' independence from Mexico. Coles was a member of Stephen F. Austin's original 300 families, and his cedar log and frame cabin, built in 1824, stands just east of town.

When Brenham won election as the county seat by two votes, Independence began a century-long slide into obscurity. Today, it is a mecca for Texana lovers with its old stone church and historic ruins.

WHERE TO GO

Independence Baptist Church. At the intersection of FM-50 and FM-390. Organized in 1839, the church's present stone building was finished in 1872 and still has services every Sunday. Sam Houston saw the light here and was baptized in nearby Rocky Creek. 409-836-5117.

Texas Baptist Historical Center. Adjacent to the Independence Baptist Church. Pre-Civil War artifacts as well as old church and family records are treasures here. Mrs. Sam Houston (Margaret Moffet Lea) and her mother are buried across the street, and the old church bell has a new stone tower on the grounds. Open Wednesday-Sunday. Free. 409-836-5117.

Old Baylor Park and Ruins of Old Baylor University. One-half mile west of the church on FM-390. This birth site of Baylor University now is marked only by a few ghostly columns and some old oaks, a nice place to picnic and enjoy the countryside. The Coles cabin has been relocated here and can be viewed by arrangement. Just ask at the church, the historical center, or at the preacher's house.

Houston Homesites. Across from Old Baylor Park. A large granite marker shows where Sam's place once stood. His wife's 1863 home (private and occupied) stands one block east of the church on the south side of FM-390.

WANDERING THE BACKROADS

Independence is the last stop on this day trip, but you easily can extend your travels. Following FM-390 east brings you to T-105. Turn northeast (left) and you can tour Washington-on-the-Brazos, Navasota, and Anderson (Trip 5, this sector). An alternate is to continue south from Independence on FM-390 to T-105 and Brenham, connecting there with either FM-389 and Trips 4 and 5 in the west sector or with T-36 south to Bellville and home.

WEST

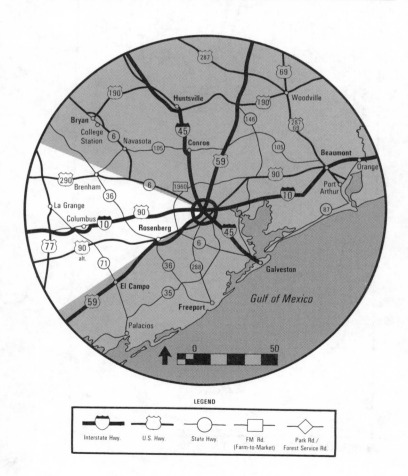

287

69

190 Huntsville 190 Woodville

Bryan 146 287
College 69
Station 6 Navasota 105 45 Conroe 105 Beaumont
59 Orange
290 Brenham 6 1960 90 Port
La Grange 36 10 Arthur
Columbus 90 87
77 10 Rosenberg 6
90 45
alt. 71 36 288 Galveston
El Campo 35 Gulf of Mexico
59 Freeport
Palacios

0   50

LEGEND

Interstate Hwy.   U.S. Hwy.   State Hwy.   FM Rd.   Park Rd. /
(Farm-to-Market) Forest Service Rd.

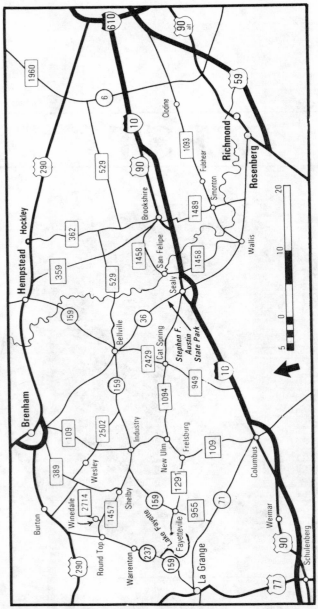

West: Day Trips 1, 3, 4 and 5

Day Trip 1

BROOKSHIRE
SAN FELIPE
SEALY
CAT SPRING

BROOKSHIRE

As you begin this day trip by driving west on I-10, consider stopping in the Katy area for these three reasons:

Para-planing. You too can hit those airways at 26 mph, strapped firmly onto a platform and propelled by two small gasoline-powered engines. As the air currents fill that parachute behind you, you rise as much as 500 feet off the ground. Safe, but for the stout of heart only. After three hours of instruction, you'll solo — all in one day. Takeoff is from Katy Park. For information, call Aero-Flight Hobby Shop, 17420 W. Little York (1.5 miles west of T-6 in the Bear Creek area). 713-463-8855.

Texas Lite-Flite, Inc. 27715 Katy Freeway, Katy. Open daily from 9 A.M. until dark, this firm offers complete instruction and equipment for flying ultra-light airplanes from their own field. For the curious but timid, there's a two-hour introductory course followed by a 30-minute ride. Advance appointments necessary. 713-392-9000.

Great Southwest Equestrian Center. Three miles south on Mason Rd. from I-10. This 107-acre, multi-million dollar facility welcomes visitors as well as dedicated horse lovers. In addition to local and national horse shows and arena polo, they host horse sales and auctions and offer both equestrian training and a livery stable with fine rental horses. The bridle trails ramble through neighboring Barker Reservoir, a chance to see natural Houston as it was before development. There's a special riding program for the handicapped, plus you can learn everything from carriage driving and steer roping to polo and Olympic-quality English-style horsemanship. In addition to a good tack shop, there's a custom saddle maker here too, a close look at an old craft. Groups can arrange barbecues, country dances, pony and hayrides. 2501 S. Mason Rd., Katy 77450. 713-578-PONY (7669).

If you drive west on T-10, Brookshire is fun to explore en route to Columbus or on a drive into the Fulshear-Simonton-Eagle Lake area (Trip 2, this sector).

Brookshire's history is brief. It was a small railroad community established in the early 1880s to serve a rich agricultural area. Its ethnic past ranges from Polish to German, Greek to Czech, Swiss to Armenian. The Waller County Festival is an energetic melding of these cultures every October.

WHERE TO GO

The Waller County Historical Museum. Fifth and Cooper streets. Built in 1910, this museum houses period furnishings, historical artifacts and documents, plus some interesting old photos. Free, but donations are welcome. Open weekdays, except Thursday. 713-934-2826.

Green Meadows Farm. Five miles north of Brookshire on FM-359. Robert and Coni Keyes welcome you to this 52-acre recreation/education farm with a two-hour tour, after which you can wander on your own, picnic, or walk the nature trails. Activities include pony rides, egg-gathering, a milking demonstration, and hayrides. From September 20 through Halloween you can pick your pumpkin from the field. Children are welcome, but no pets. Open daily, March 15-December 15, except Easter and Thanksgiving. Fee. Information: P.O. Box 547, Brookshire 77423. 713-391-7995.

Lilipons Water Gardens. Just south of I-10 on FM-1489. Where else in Houston do you find acres of exotic goldfish amid blooming lotus and water lilies? The shop sells everything needed to create your own water garden, but visitors are welcome to just browse among the 25 production ponds out back. These folks also publish a large color catalog (fee) and even mail goldfish. Free; □. 713-934-8525.

WHERE TO EAT

The Cotton Gin. The intersection of US-90 and FM-359 at Bains Street. This restaurant is reason enough to come to Brookshire. Built in 1936, it hummed with activity as a working gin for a decade before closing down in 1946 due to a decline in area cotton production. Much of the equipment had come from an earlier Brookshire gin built on another site by T.A. Trettin in the 1920s. Today, that old equipment is part of the restaurant's authentic decor.

In 1979 some Brookshire natives, Harris and Jo Ann Garrett, bought the ramshackle old building, put the family to work refurbishing the place, and opened it as a restaurant. The menu ranges from beef, pork, and chicken to seafood, and the house specialty is Eli's Encore, an ice cream dessert topped with a hot sauce made of peach brandy and preserves. You'll find a bar and a grandchildren's room — nice to know if you're in need of either one. $$; □. Open Monday-Saturday for lunch and dinner; Sunday for dinner only. 713-391-4034.

WANDERING THE BACKROADS

If you are coming from the FM-1960/T-6 area of Houston, swing west on FM-529 and then south on FM-362 to Brookshire. Going home, just reverse those directions to miss the traffic crunch on T-6 near Bear Creek.

If you love country drives, save some time for wandering south of I-10 on FM-1489. This is horse and cotton-growing country, and the ranches and farms are beautiful. This road passes through the small communities of Simonton, Wallis, and East Bernard, an excellent route into the southwestern sector of this book.

SAN FELIPE

To reach San Felipe, continue west from Brookshire on I-10 for 8 miles and watch for the exit signs to Stephen F. Austin State Park.

Alas, how fleeting fame. From 1823 to 1836, this community collected a string of "firsts" that earned it a secure niche in Texas history. Then known as San Felipe de Austin, it was the original settlement and capital of Stephen F. Austin's first colony. It also was the site of the first Anglo newspaper and postal system, and the founding spot of the Texas Rangers. The town was burned in 1836 to prevent its use by the advancing Mexican army. Although rebuilt later in that decade, it never regained its original momentum.

In addition to visiting the oldest post office in Texas, visitors today find some pieces of San Felipe's past in the historical portion of Stephen F. Austin State Park. Traces of wagon ruts still lead to the old ferry crossing on the Brazos River, located inside the park boundaries.

A dog-run log cabin is a replica of Austin's headquarters, but the J.J. Josey Store, built in 1847 and later restored as a museum, has been closed due to vandalism. The park is open daily, year-round, and also offers picnicking, camping, swimming, golf, and numerous other family activities. Take the Stephen F. Austin exit (FM-1458) from I-10 and go 2.2 miles north to the park entrance.

After looping through the park, return to I-10 and continue west to the Sealy exit.

SEALY

San Felipe sold a portion of its original 22,000-acre township to the Gulf, Colorado, and Santa Fe Railroad in the 1870s to create the town of Sealy in 1879. That town now bills itself as the "best little hometown in Texas" and collects a few more refugee Houstonians every month.

Visitors enjoy the drive down oak-shaded Fifth Street with its turn-of-the-century homes and around the downtown sector which is being restored to its original appearance.

Every July 4 there's a Sealy-bration in the Lion's Club City Park, and September brings Western Days, complete with parade, carnival, music including oompah bands, flea market, antique show and sale, etc. Nearby, the small Czech community of Frydek (pop. 150) celebrates its ethnic heritage every spring.

For information on San Felipe, Sealy, or Frydek, contact the Sealy Chamber of Commerce, P.O. Box 586, Sealy 77474. 409-885-3222.

WHERE TO GO

Port City Stockyards. North of Sealy on T-36. This is one of the largest cattle auction operations in America, and visitors are welcome. Hogs are auctioned on Monday mornings and cattle on Wednesday mornings, year-round, and the cafeteria adjoining is one of the best places to eat in Sealy, particularly for Tex-Mex. Open weekdays. $-$$. Stockyards, 409-885-3526; cafe, 409-885-2831.

CAT SPRING

When the wildflowers bloom in late March and early April, this tidy crossroads community looks like a calendar picture. From Sealy, take FM-1094 north toward New Ulm. Just past the intersection with FM-949 (to Columbus) watch for an unusual eight-sided building on a rise to your right. This is the Cat Spring Agricultural Society Hall, built in 1902 and still the heart of community activities today.

The Cat Spring Agricultural Society was founded in 1856 and is considered the forerunner of today's Texas Agricultural Extension Service. Early German and Czech farmers pooled their knowledge through this society, keeping explicit planting and production records on their small cotton and grain farms in a central book. All entries were written in German until America entered the First World War. The practice was then deemed unwise, and all records thereafter were written in English. They still are in use as a reference by local farmers.

Visitors are welcome to whirl around the Agricultural Hall's dance floor on the first Saturday night of every month. The music ranges from today's country and western tunes to the traditional waltzes, polkas, and schottische. The first Sunday in June annually is the June Feast, complete with a barbecue and election of a queen to reign for the next 25 years.

WANDERING THE BACKROADS

From Cat Spring, you have several choices. A left turn on FM-949 at its intersection with FM-1094 will scoot you southwest through pretty country to I-10. A turn west then takes you to Columbus; a turn east returns you to Houston.

An alternate route takes you northwest to New Ulm on FM-1094 and then southwest into Frelsburg via FM-109. From Frelsburg, you can either continue south on FM-109 to Columbus (Trip 3, this sector), or you can go northwest on FM-1291 to Fayetteville (Trip 4, this sector).

If you haven't yet explored to the north, consider taking FM-949 and FM-2429 from Cat Spring northeast to Bellville (Trip 5, this sector). Continue north on T-36 to Brenham (Trip 6, northwest sector).

This entire area is threaded with small FM and county roads, and rambling is a joy. But be sure you have a good state highway map in hand if you really care where you end up.

Day Trip 2

**FULSHEAR
SIMONTON
EAGLE LAKE**

(See map, p. 55)

FULSHEAR

This short day trip on I-10 west is ideal if you like beautiful country, rodeo, good hunting, and meat — not necessarily in that order.

The crossroads town of Fulshear has earned a strong local reputation for good barbecue, thanks to Dozier's. You can buy it either by the pound or to go, and Mr. Dozier will be glad to take you out back and show you how they make sausage and smoke their meats. Lest you should think this place is just like another BBQ place, be aware that they sell more than 3000 lbs. of brisket, 300 lbs. of sausage, and 500 lbs. of pork ribs every week. Open daily. $. 713-346-1411. From I-10 west, take FM-359 south about 7 miles and watch for Dozier's sign. From west Houston you can continue out Westheimer to Fulshear and turn right at the blinking light on the FM-359 intersection. Dozier's is three blocks north on your left.

SIMONTON

The big attraction here is the Roundup Rodeo, held every Saturday night year-round at the indoor arena. Anyone with the entry money can compete in everything from bareback riding and barrel racing to roping and bulldogging. There's a calf and goat scramble for the kids, and a barbecue dinner to start things off.

Dinner service opens at 6 p.m. $; □. The rodeo is at 8:30 p.m. Tickets are available at the door for both. From Fulshear, continue

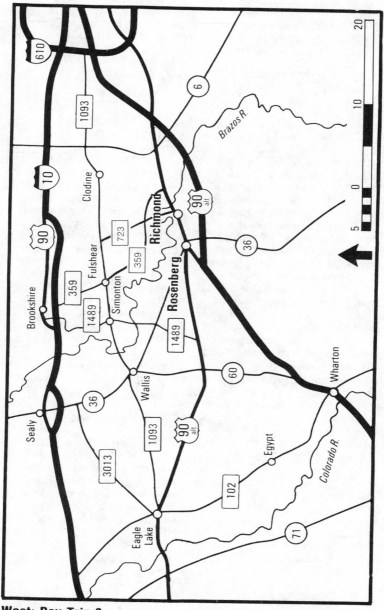

West: Day Trip 2

west on FM-1093 five miles to Simonton. From I-10 west, take the FM-1489 exit in Brookshire south for 10 miles to Simonton. Turn right on FM-1093 (blinking light) to the arena. Call 713-346-1534.

EAGLE LAKE

Continuing west from Simonton on FM-1093 about 27 miles brings you to Eagle Lake. As to how this community got its name, you can go Gothic or plain vanilla. The Gothic version says that a Karankawa Indian maiden named Prairie Flower had two suitors, Light Foot and Leap High. Unable to decide between them, she challenged them to bring down a young eaglet from a nest in a cottonwood by a natural lake. Light Foot did and won the fair maiden's hand, whereupon poor Leap High decamped in high dudgeon to the nearby Colorado River.

The less romantic tale is that two of Austin's first settlers shot an eagle on the shores of this lake in 1823, and it was thereafter called Eagle Lake. Whatever, the lake is still the main feature of this small town. Unfortunately, it is private and you have to be a hunter on a guided trip to enjoy it.

The Eagle Lake community actually was settled in 1851, and today it thrives as the "Goose Hunting Capital of the World." Day trippers can arrange hunts through a number of guides; a list is available from the Eagle Lake Chamber of Commerce, P. O. Box 216, Eagle Lake 77434. 409-234-2780. That mailing address translates to 100 East Main if you already are in town. Open weekdays only.

There is some good fishing in assorted gravel pits around Eagle Lake, but most are on private property and hard to find. For information, contact Johnny's Sport Shop, 101 Booth Dr., Eagle Lake 77434. 409-234-2956. Open Monday-Saturday.

WHERE TO GO

Attwater Prairie Chicken National Wildlife Refuge. Six miles northeast of Eagle Lake on the west side of FM-3013. This 8,000-acre refuge is the happy "booming" grounds for this nearly extinct bird, and day visitors can follow 12 miles of road through the prairie preserve. Best time to go is during the booming season, mid-February through April. Each male prairie chicken has his own domain and protects it with a war dance. Reservations are needed to use the photo blinds, and binoculars are highly desirable. To find the best observation spot, stop at the main office just inside the entrance to the refuge and ask directions. Open year-round. Visitors are encouraged to call in advance for advice. P. O. Box 518, Eagle Lake 77434. 409-234-3021.

WHERE TO EAT

The Farris 1912. 201 North McCarty at Post Office Street. Constructed as the Hotel Dallas in 1912, this building flourished until the depression, and then floundered into disrepair and virtual abandonment. Thanks to the restoration efforts of Bill and Helyn Farris, who bought it in 1974, this former flophouse is now a fun hotel and restaurant. Opened for guests again in 1977, it is spacious and comfortable, with 16 bedrooms, a huge second floor sitting room/mezzanine, and assorted public parlours. Stop in for a look or a meal, even if you can't stay.

Food is served in the Drummer's Room daily during November, December, and January, starting with a goose hunter's breakfast in the early morning. Lunch features daily specials and a buffet, and dinner offers seafood, steaks, and other entrees. February through October, the hotel's antique and gift shop is open weekdays but meals are served only to tour groups, clubs, and private parties. The Farris family also owns eight acres on the eastern shore of Eagle Lake which they make available to guests for bird-watching and sunset appreciation. The entire Eagle Lake area is prized by Audubon members. $$$. □. 409-234-2546.

WANDERING THE BACKROADS

From Eagle Lake, you can return to Houston by reversing your entry route: FM-1093 east to home. Alternates: take FM-102 north to I-10 and jog west a few miles to Columbus (Trip 3, this sector) or take FM-102 south to Wharton (Trip 1, southwest sector) and turn north on US-59 to Richmond-Rosenberg (Trip 2, southwest sector).

Day Trip 3

COLUMBUS
FRELSBURG
NEW ULM

(See map, p. 48)

COLUMBUS

Some 56 miles west of Houston's city limits via I-10, Columbus is in one of the oldest inhabited areas of the state. The early Spanish maps of Texas marked this as a sizeable Indian village known as Montezuma, and Stephen F. Austin's first colonists called it Beason's Ferry. Today, as Columbus, it is one of the prettiest and most historic towns in Texas. As you stroll through the shady town square, it's hard to believe that the busy interstate zips by less than 1 mile to the south.

Back in 1823 Stephen F. Austin brought a survey party to this fertile land looped by the Colorado River, thinking it would make a fine headquarters and capital for his first settlement. The river was deep enough for commerce, and the busy Atascosito Trail crossed the river nearby. But this was Karankawa country — a fierce Indian tribe labeled by history as cannibals — and the threat made the existing settlement in San Felipe a better choice.

Some of Austin's colony did settle here, however, and a tiny village named Columbus was laid out in 1835. Its life was brief. In March of 1836, Sam Houston and his forces retreated from Gonzales and camped in Columbus on the east bank of the Colorado River. The pursuing Mexican Army settled in on the west bank where it soon was reinforced by additional troops.

Knowing his position was weak and an attack on the Mexicans would be suicide for both his men and the cause of Texas independence, Houston elected to retreat further. Moving on to Hempstead (Trip 4, northwest sector), he ordered all the buildings in and around Columbus burned so that they would be of no use to the Mexicans. Caught in the middle, local residents fled east to safety, a migration termed by history as "the Runaway Scrape."

Houston's strategy was vindicated by his victory over Santa Anna and the Mexican Army at San Jacinto the following month, and slowly, Columbus began to build again. Today, it is a delightful town full of live oak and magnolia trees. Thanks to large natural deposits of sand and gravel, Columbus literally is "where Houston comes from." Approximately 90 percent of the aggregate used to construct Houston's skyscrapers was excavated nearby.

The town's mainstay always has been the river on its doorstep. Early settlers floated their construction lumber downstream from pine forests near Bastrop, and by the mid-19th century, paddle wheelers were making regular runs between Columbus, Austin, and Matagorda. Dressed up with names like the Moccasin Belle, Flying Jenny, and the Kate Ward, these flat bottom boats also carried cotton from large plantations south of town to the shipping docks at Matagorda Bay (Trip 1, southwest sector).

Today, the river still figures in the town's life, but with a lighter touch. Columbus children grow up "floating round the bend," and local high school seniors traditionally celebrate graduation with all-night float trips. The most popular stretch for recreation starts at the north river bridge (T-71 north) to east river bridge (US-90), a distance of about ½ mile by land and 7 miles and four hours by water. You'll need two cars, one of which should be parked near the east river bridge.

Wide and smooth, with only a few small rapids, the Colorado River at Columbus is relatively safe for novice canoeists. The numerous long sandbars make night floats a timeless experience. Moonlight glows from these freshwater beaches, and the wildlife show is fascinating as the river comes alive with beaver, deer, and raccoons.

Exploring Columbus is easy with the Historical Trailguide published by the Columbus Chamber of Commerce. It is available at the chamber offices on the ground floor of the Stafford Opera House (Spring Street, across from Courthouse Square) or by mail: P. O. Box 343, Columbus 78934. 409-732-5881. Open Monday-Friday. There are 44 historical medallions and four Texas Centennial markers in town, although the vast majority mark private residences which are open to the public only during the Magnolia Homes Tour.

Among the best candidates for a windshield tour are the Tate-Senftenberg-Brandon House (1860s), 616 Walnut; Raumonda (1887), 1100 Bowie; the Alley Log Cabin (1836), 1230 Bowie; Dilue Harris House (1860), 602 Washington; and the Youens-Hopkins House (1860), 617 Milam.

WHERE TO GO

The Colorado County Courthouse. Bounded by Spring, Milam, Walnut, and Travis streets on Courthouse Square. Built during 1890 and 1891, this is the third courthouse on the same site and still is the county seat. The four-faced clock is original, but its steeple fell in a 1909 hurricane and was replaced by a neoclassic dome. A full restoration was completed in 1980 and uncovered a handsome stained-glass dome above the district courtroom, hidden for generations under a false ceiling. The courthouse is open Monday-Friday.

Take special note of the famous Courthouse Oak, 2,000 years old and the site of the first district court held in 1837. At that time the first courthouse on this site had been burned by Houston's forces, and a second one had yet to be built. Judge R. M. Williamson, known as "three-legged Willie" because of his false leg, elected to hear cases under this tree.

Confederate Memorial Hall Museum. On the southwest corner of Courthouse Square. This old water tower was built 400,000 bricks strong in 1883. Dynamite didn't dent it in a later demolition attempt, so the United Daughters of the Confederacy decided it was a safe repository for their treasures. The exhibits feature clothing, small possessions, articles, documents, and pictures of early Columbus, including artifacts from the "Old Three Hundred," as Stephen F. Austin's first colony was known. Open only by appointment, and donations are appreciated. 409-732-2571 or 409-732-5269.

Koliba Home Museum. 1124 Front St. This 18-room private home is as interesting as its contents. The original portion of the house was built between 1837 and 1838 and has been expanded in sections over the years. The latest addition is a large office, added in 1958 by former State Representative Homer Koliba and his wife. The family's personal collection of antiques and Texana is extensive, well-organized, and labeled. The back garden has a "bottle forest," old-time barber and blacksmith shops, and a toolshed filled with parts for horseless carriages. Fee. Open daily. 409-732-2913.

Stafford Bank and Opera House. On Spring Street, across from Courthouse Square. Built by millionaire cattleman R. E. Stafford in 1886 for a reputed $50,000, this elegant old building originally housed Stafford's bank on the first floor and a 1,000 seat theatre upstairs. Headliners such as Lillian Russell and Al Jolson performed here, and the original 15-foot crystal chandelier soon will shine again with the restoration of the theatre. So far, only the bottom floor of the building has been spiffed up. Don't miss the unusual marble cornerstone. Open Monday-Friday, and during the Magnolia Homes Tour.

Grave of the Infidel. Odd Fellows Rest Cemetery on Montezuma Street. Like all frontiers, the Columbus area attracted characters. Back in the 1890s, Ike Towell made a name for himself as an outspoken atheist. The town marshall, he also is credited with the establishment of the "Jim Crow" law in the area. He wrote his own funeral service, and his tombstone reads "Here lies Ike Towell, an infidel, who had no hope of heaven or fear of hell."

The Quail Farm. FM-949 turn-off of I-10 and then north for ½ mile. This family operation sells Northern Bob White Quail, dead or alive. Visitors are welcome to view growing birds inside fly pens in one building. Freshly killed, non-frozen quail are sold only while butchering is going on, so call in advance if that is what you want. Otherwise only frozen quail are sold at the farm. Information: Route 2, Box 181, Columbus 78934. 409-732-3880.

Hunting. Colorado County is happy hunting grounds for deer, quail, dove, and geese. Every winter it becomes the goose capital of the world because of its location on the Mississippi flyway. Arrangements to hunt can be made through the following: Clifton Tyler (goose and wild duck guide; day and season hunting), 101 S. River Dr., Columbus 78934, 409-732-2414, or Francis Truchard (deer, duck, goose, dove, quail guide; day and season hunting), R.R. Box 2014, Columbus 78934, 409-732-6849.

WHERE TO EAT

Schobel's Restaurant. 2020 Milam. This family restaurant cuts its own steaks, grinds its own hamburger, and makes its own pies. The menu also includes seafood and Mexican dishes, and there's a large buffet for daily lunch and again on Friday night. $$; □. 409-732-2385.

Mikeska's Barbeque. 519 Walnut. Justifiably known as the BBQ king of the southwest to local folks. Open Monday-Saturday for lunch and dinner. $. 409-732-3101.

WANDERING THE BACKROADS

Columbus is the gateway to all of Austin and Fayette counties, rolling farmland that still looks much as it did when it was settled by Polish, German, and Czech immigrants in the 1800s. FM-949 north to Cat Spring is a nice, rural drive, and FM-109 north continues this day trip to the small German communities of Frelsburg and New Ulm.

FRELSBURG

When you stop to chat in this region, don't be surprised to hear strong German accents. The ethnic heritage of this community, north on FM-109, runs deep. The town is named for John and William Frels who settled here in the 1830s.

You'll see Saints Peter and Paul Catholic Church on a hill as you approach town on FM-109. Although this particular sanctuary was built in 1927, this Catholic parish is the oldest in Texas, organized in 1847. Visitors are welcome, either for mass or to look at the three carved wood altars. Nearby St. John's Lutheran Church recently celebrated its centennial.

Heinsohen's General Store has served the area for generations. Stop in for a cool drink, and you'll find it stocks everything from the latest in electronic games to pegged pants.

The big doin's in Frelsburg is the annual Fireman's Picnic on the second weekend in June. A fund-raiser, it also is an enjoyable look at a small German community in the heart of Texas.

From Frelsburg, continue north on FM-109 to the more sizeable community of New Ulm, population 650.

NEW ULM

Also founded by Germans, Czechs, and Poles in the early 1800s, New Ulm soon may be in for its second golden age. Back in the 1940s the entrepreneurial Glenn McCarthy made some big Texas bucks in the nearby Frelsburg oil field and brought lots of his Hollywood friends to the quiet streets of New Ulm. Today, new wells are bringing another wave of prosperity and activity of a more historic nature.

The Jeanne and John Blocker Foundation has been quietly buying log cabins and old homes and moving them from area farms onto five acres on FM-1094 at the eastern edge of town. Although it probably will be several years before the restorations are complete and open to the public, you are welcome to drive by and watch the progress. At this writing, the foundation owns 22 old structures, built between 1845 and 1890. Many of them are wooden cottages typical of those built on the small German farms around New Ulm during the latter half of the 19th century. Almost all were in threatened condition on their original sites, doomed to disappear from neglect or demolition.

WHERE TO EAT

The Tavern. One block south of the intersection of FM-109 and FM-1094. This is an institution in Austin County, known for its thick hamburgers and a chicken-fried steak that hangs off both ends of the plate. Steaks, chicken, and fresh seafood too, including oysters, catfish, and codfish. Open for lunch and dinner daily except on the first Monday of every month. $-$$. 409-992-3450.

The Parlour. Front Street. They serve steak, but the house specialty is fresh seafood and homemade desserts. They also feature a second type of "Austin County Sound" when a local homemade band tunes up the wash tub, rake, accordian, and musical saw for a go at C&W and old German tunes. Set-ups and eight kinds of draft beer are served in this former funeral parlour where you can belly-up to an antique marble bar. This is one of the oldest operating buildings (circa 1893) in Austin County. Open for lunch Friday-Sunday, dinner Tuesday-Sunday. The weekend lunch buffet is a bargain, all you can eat. $-$$. 409-992-3499.

WANDERING THE BACKROADS

To reach Houston from New Ulm, go east 23 miles on FM-1094 to Sealy and then east on I-10 to home.

If you want to extend the day trip, you have several choices. From New Ulm, take FM-109 north to Industry and its intersection with T-159. A turn west (left) and then a jog northwest on FM-1457 takes you to Round Top (Trip 5, this sector); a turn east (right) on T-159 brings you to Bellville (also Trip 5, this sector).

Day Trip 4

LA GRANGE
FAYETTEVILLE

(See map, p. 48)

LA GRANGE

There are two ways to get to La Grange from Houston, but they both follow I-10 west some 56 miles to Columbus. There you can either take T-71 northwest 26 miles to La Grange, or continue on the interstate another 21 miles to the US-77 turn-off and go north 17 miles to your destination. The latter way covers two sides of a triangle but takes you through the two small German towns of Schulenburg and Weimar. You might want to stop and visit some before exploring La Grange.

Long before Marvin Zindler focused the bright lights of publicity and traditional morality on Miss Mona and her Chicken Ranch *(Best Little Whorehouse in Texas)* a few years ago, La Grange had a colorful personality. A bear of a man known as Strap Buckner was running an Indian trading post here by 1819, and local legend says he cleared the townsite of La Grange by a wild wrestling match with Satan.

Whatever the truth, a small community began about 1831 where the La Bahia Trail crossed the Colorado River, and some of Stephen F. Austin's first colony helped tame the land. By 1837 the town known as La Grange was the seat of government for Fayette County. Today the courthouse, built in 1855, still stands in the town square, and the original clock still works and chimes on the hour.

Pause for a moment under Muster Oak on the square's northeast corner. Traditionally, through six conflicts starting with the Mexican attack of 1842, La Grange's able-bodied men have gathered here with their families before leaving for battle.

WHERE TO GO

Hermes Drug Store. Across from the courthouse at 148 North Washington. Established in 1856, this is the oldest drug store in continuous operation in Texas. Visitors can see authentic old-time

63

fixtures, beveled mirrors, and more. Open Monday-Saturday. 409-968-3357.

N.W. Faison Home, Museum, and Garden Center. 822 South Jefferson St. The nucleus of this gracious frontier home is a two-room cabin built of pine around 1845. Bought in 1866 by N.W. Faison, a Fayette County clerk and land surveyor who survived the Dawson Massacre, the home remained in the Faison family until 1960. Now owned by the La Grange Garden Club, the home is interesting for its graceful frontier architecture, antique furnishings, and artifacts from the Mexican War. Fee. Open weekends. March through September.

Fayette County Heritage Museum and Library. 855 South Jefferson St., across from the Faison home. A local Bicentennial project, the museum has special humidified archives to preserve historic documents. Free. Open daily, but hours vary. 409-968-6418.

St. James Episcopal Church. 156 North Monroe. Built in 1885 and still painted its original rust and cream, this small church has its original furnishings, handmade by the rector and his congregation. Visitors are welcome at the 10 a.m. Sunday service. 409-968-3910.

Monument Hill State Historic Site. Two miles south of town off US-77. Even after the Texans' historic victory over the Mexican forces at San Jacinto, the Mexican army continued to raid this portion of Texas through the next decade. The tragic 1842 sagas of the Dawson Massacre near San Antonio and the ill-fated Mier Expedition are the focus of this memorial. Both are lesser known but interesting chapters of Lone Star history.

This popular picnic site, high on a bluff overlooking the Colorado River, has one trail designed for the handicapped and a nature walk through the woods. In 1978 the adjacent Kreische Brewery and homesite were added to the facility, and restoration has progressed enough to allow visitors to walk those grounds. Kreische, who was a skilled stone mason and brewer from Europe, established this first brewery in Texas between 1860 and 1870 below his home on what is now Monument Hill. Ultimately it became the third-largest brewery in the state, and his product, a dark brew called Frisch Auf, was sold at his beer garden. The restoration has cleaned out the springs that provided water for the brewery and stabilized the old buildings. Open daily. Fee. P.O. Box C, La Grange 78945. 409-968-5658.

WHERE TO EAT

The Bon Ton Restaurant. T-71 east, La Grange. What started as a good but small place to eat on La Grange's Courthouse Square is now a good and large family restaurant on the main road into town. There are daily specials and a buffet, plus a regular menu that ranges through the seafood-steak-chicken standards. Emphasis is on down-home German and American food, all served with home baked bread. $$; □. Open daily. 409-968-5863.

The Cottonwood Inn. T-71 west in La Grange. True believers think this family restaurant serves the ultimate in chicken-fried steak. Locals say the rest of the menu is equally good, particularly the tenderloin strip. $$; ☐. Open daily. 409-968-5445.

Lukas Bakery. 135 North Main. The place to go in La Grange for pigs-in-the-blanket, homemade breads, rolls, and cookies. $. Closed Sunday 409-968-3052.

Weimar Country Inn. On the corner of Center and Jackson streets in Weimar, 30 miles south of La Grange adjacent to I-10, and a 15 minute drive from Columbus. This freshly restored old hotel not only will put you up for the night in antique style, it serves some of the best food and drink in south Texas. The dining room is a charmer with its pressed-tin ceiling, and there's a city park out back for the kiddies to romp in when they get restless. $$; ☐. The inn is open daily, but the restaurant is closed on Sunday afternoon, Monday and Tuesday. 409-725-8888.

Short Stop, 152 West Colorado on the La Grange town square. A local favorite for its chicken soup, this casual place specializes in home-style and Greek cooking. You'll find Blue Bell ice cream here, along with a game room for the kiddies. Purists note: everything is made from scratch from fresh food. Nothing here is canned or has artificial preservatives. Open Monday-Saturday. $-$$. 409-968-8877.

WANDERING THE BACKROADS

Your next stop on this day trip is Fayetteville. From La Grange take T-159 northeast 15 miles on its zigzag course through the countryside. Bass fishermen may want to detour east on County Road 196 to the new 2400-acre Lake Fayette, the cooling pond for the Fayette Power Project. Open year-round, it offers fishing, camping, swimming, and power boating. Fee. 409-249-5208.

After touring Fayetteville, you can continue east 30 miles on T-159 to Bellville and then home (Trip 5, this sector).

Or you can reverse the order, touring Fayetteville first and then continuing on to La Grange. See the map with this section for your route options. Either way, you can easily connect with tours of Round Top and Winedale (Trip 5, this sector) or Burton and Brenham (Trip 6, northwest sector).

If you are traveling any of these roads from late March through May, contact the La Grange Chamber of Commerce in advance. They scout the best routes for color during the wildflower season. Information: P.O. Box 70, La Grange 78945. 409-968-5756.

FAYETTEVILLE

If you like the big time and bright lights, move on. This small town keeps a low profile, tucked away in the rolling farmland east of La Grange. If too many folks fall in love with it, it's bound to change, and that would be a pity.

Some of Austin's first colony were sharp enough to settle here in the early 1820s, and by 1833 the tiny community was a stage station on the old San Felipe Trail, with services to Austin via Round Top and Bastrop. The town officially was mapped in 1847, and the next decade saw extensive German and Czech immigration, an ethnic blend that continues here today.

In the town's settlement days free food was served to all comers, but occasionally the vittles would run out before the customers did. Late arrivals were told to "lick the skillet," and Fayetteville also became known as Lickskillet as a result!

Fayetteville looks much as it did at the end of the last century: a series of two- and three-block streets in a grid with a central square. The town's pride and heart is the rare Victorian precinct courthouse in the center of that square, built in 1880 for the heady sum of $800. The four-faced clock in the steeple resulted from a ten-year fund-raising effort by the "Do Your Duty Club" and was installed with much civic horn-tooting in 1934.

City folks cherish Fayetteville as a wind-down place. The best way to get on Fayetteville-time is to pick up a walking map from one of the stores and take a slow stroll around town.

WHERE TO GO

The Red & White. On the square. Built between 1853 and 1855 as a store, it is considered the oldest building on the square. It later served as an opera house, hat shop, furniture store, and grocery (known as the Red & White, hence the current name). Today, it's a weekend project for its Houston owners and sells imported beer and wine, antiques, and assorted handicrafts. There's an old juke box with records to match, domino tables if you are looking for a game, and an antique co-op upstairs. Open Friday-Monday. 409-378-2722.

Fayetteville Emporium and the Fayetteville Workshop. Washington St. on the square. You'll find stained glass, pottery, paintings, and photography on exhibit and for sale in this combination gift shop, atelier, and gallery.

Chovaneks. Corner of Live Oak and Fayette streets, on the square. In what must be termed a Gargantuan case of overstocking, this old store still has dry goods typical of the 1940s and 1950s. When it's gone, it's gone. Open Monday-Saturday.

WHERE TO EAT

Bill & Jeanie's Country Place and Hotel. Corner of Fayette and Washington streets on the square. Built in 1900 as Zapp's Mercantile this substantial building now is a nine-room hotel with nostalgic furnishings, ceiling fans, and his and her bathrooms down the hall. An upstairs sitting room opens onto a front balcony, just right for rocking and visiting. Downstairs in the rear are the offices of noted architect Clovis Heimsath, who with his wife, Maryann, owns the hotel.

Two-week advance notice is recommended, although there usually are rooms available for mid-week drop-ins. Open daily, whenever someone is around to answer the phone or a knock on the door.

The **Country Place Restaurant** is on the premises. Although Jean serves breakfast daily if there are guests in the hotel, the restaurant officially is open from Friday-Monday. Friday nights feature Mexican gourmet goodies, and Saturday brings inventive country fare. Sunday and Monday are table d'hote — whatever she feels like fixing. She grows her own vegetables and buys local meat and milk. Lunches feature soup and salad buffets, and coffee and cake are available throughout the afternoon. Beer and wine are served, and all desserts are homemade. $-$$. 409-783-2396 for both hotel and dinner reservations.

The Lickskillet Inn. One-half block north of the square on Fayette Street. Built in 1853, this is believed to be the oldest home in Fayetteville. True or not, it certainly is one of the most hospitable. Owners Steve and Jeanette Donaldson rent cozy rooms furnished in antiques, some of which are for sale. In addition to heat and ceiling fans, the rooms have air conditioners and pot-bellied stoves, and the bath is at the end of the enclosed central hall. The modest rate covers a double-bed room and continental breakfast. Evening meals are available with advance notice and feature home-grown seasonal vegetables. No children or pets, please, plus smoking is not allowed indoors. $$; □. Information: P.O. Box 85, Fayetteville 78940. 409-378-2846.

Day Trip 5

ROUND TOP
WINEDALE
BELLVILLE

(See map, p. 48)

ROUND TOP

Begin this day trip by driving northwest from Houston on US-290. Shortly after you pass the small town of Burton swing south on T-237 and slow down to enjoy the lovely countryside that still looks much as it did 150 years ago.

When it comes to vintage Texas villages that have retained the essence of their past, Round Top is the champ. Officially founded in 1835 by settlers from Stephen F. Austin's second colony, it was first called Jones Post Office and then Townsend, after the five Townsend families who established plantations in the area. The name of Round Top first applied to a stage stop 2 miles north, a landmark by 1847 because it had a house with a round top. When the stage line between Houston and Austin moved its route slightly to the south, the town and the name followed.

Driving into Round Top is like passing through an invisible time warp. A small white meeting house in the middle of the village green is part of the town's charm. In fact, Round Top is so small, so compact and neat, that visitors often feel like giants abroad in Lilliput land.

Those first Anglo settlers were followed by Germans, many of whom were intellectuals oppressed in their native country. Others were skilled carpenters and stone masons whose craftsmanship marks numerous buildings that survive today. A drive on the lanes around Round Top is a lesson in enduring architecture.

With its current population of 87, Round Top holds two distinctions. Not only is it the smallest incorporated town in the state, it has what many think is the oldest Fourth of July celebration west of the

Mississippi. Since 1826 local folks have been kicking up their heels on Independence Day, and the annual tradition now runs to orations, barbecues, a trial ride, and the firing of the cannon in the town square.

Whenever you visit, just park your car near the square and walk around. Round Top folks welcome visitors and have lots of tales to tell, so stop and chat as you explore.

WHERE TO GO

Moore's Fort. Across T-237 from the town square. Look for a double log cabin with an open dog-trot center, and you've found the frontier home of John Henry Moore. Built about 1828 near the Colorado River in La Grange, it was used primarily as a defense against Indians. It was moved to Round Top and restored several years ago. Free. Open daily, afternoons only.

Bethlehem Lutheran Church. Up the hill from Moore's Fort and one block southwest. This sturdy stone church was dedicated in 1866 and is in use still. The front door usually is unlocked, so climb the narrow wood stairs to the loft. Not only will you get a strong feel for the simplicity of the old days, you'll see an unusual pipe organ, one of several built of cedar in the 1860s for area Lutheran churches by a local craftsman, Johann Traugott Wantke. The old churchyard cemetery is charming and ageless, enclosed by a hand-laid stone wall reminiscent of New England. Open daily. Free.

Round Top General Store. On the T-237 side of the town square. Not every hardware store serves beer, but this one does! That's what comes with being the gathering place for a predominately German community since 1847. Open Wednesday-Sunday, but hours are "very uncertain," according to owner Betty Schatte. 409-249-3600.

Henkel Square. On the square. Back in 1852, a German immigrant named Edward A. Henkel bought 25 acres in Round Top to establish a mercantile store. The following year he built a two-story home that today is the keystone of Henkel Square, a historical open-air museum operated by the Texas Pioneer Arts Foundation.

Dedicated to preserving the history of this region, Henkel Square is a collection of 13 historically important structures scattered across eight acres of pasture in the heart of town. The docents are local ladies who explain each home or building, its furnishings, and how it fit into early Texas life. Don't miss the old Lutheran Church, which doubled as a school. Its painted motto translates from German to: "I call the living to my church and the dead to their graves," a reference to its two-clapper bell. One rings, the other tolls.

Five of the buildings were moved to Henkel Square from sites in surrounding communities, and the lumber needed for restorations was cut in the local woods, just as it was in pioneer times. Using old tools and techniques, today's craftsmen have kept each structure faithful to its period, an attention to authenticity that has won Henkel Square awards for restoration excellence.

The entrance is through an old Victorian building that used to be

Round Top's drug store, and several of the homes have outstanding wall stenciling and period furniture. Open daily except major holidays. Fee. Information: P. O. Box 82, Round Top 78954. 409-249-3308.

Henkel Square also owns the Yellow Cottage two blocks away, which can be rented for the night. Call the above number for information.

Festival Hill. One-half mile north of the town square on T-237. What once was rolling, open pasture now is a mecca for music lovers throughout the world. Back in 1968 noted pianist James Dick performed near Round Top and fell victim to its bucolic charm. Returning in 1971, he held the first of his musical festival-institutes in a small school building, a venture that grew into permanent quarters on Festival Hill in 1976. Every summer 60 music students attend master classes taught by the professional guest faculty, often performing with internationally known musicians in a series of public open-air concerts.

Two handsome old homes have been moved onto the grounds. The William Lockhart Clayton house, built in 1870 in La Grange, is now staff living quarters, and the C. A. Menke House, originally an old ranch house in Hempstead, is the new conference center. Limited overnight accommodations are available by advance reservation from August through April.

An early June weekend gala opens the summer concert series, and many weekend concerts are offered from August to April. Tickets can be purchased at the box office the night of the performance, except for the Interlude series on Sunday afternoons. There usually is a free concert for children in mid-June.

Picnic box lunches and dinners can be ordered for the summer performances, and gourmet dinners are served by reservation only on Saturday nights for the August through April series. Information: Festival Hill, P. O. Box 89, Round Top 78954. 409-249-3129.

WHERE TO EAT

Round Top Cafe. On the square. Mr. Birkelbach served up his special brand of barbecue here for years, and new owners continue the tradition on Saturday and Sunday. They also serve a memorable plate lunch and a full menu of steaks, sandwiches and salads. Frills run to Blue Bell ice cream cones, wine and keg beer, homemade breads and kolaches, and desserts made by a local German lady. All veggies are locally grown, and Friday is buttermilk fried chicken day, worth remembering when you plan your Round Top trip. Open for lunch and dinner Tuesday through Sunday, plus lunch on Monday. $-$$. 409-249-3611.

The Oaks. Five miles south of Round Top on the east side of T-237. Some 36 oak trees shade this quiet family restaurant, noted for its fresh seafood. Thursday is shrimp and fried catfish time, and during the season the oysters and shrimp are fresh from Port Lavaca. Open for dinner only, Thursday-Saturday. $$. 409-249-3741.

WANDERING THE BACKROADS

After seeing Round Top, continue this day trip by following FM-1457 north from the northeast corner of the town square. After 4 miles, watch for the FM-2714 turn-off, a short lane into Winedale.

If you have lingered too long in Round Top and must head home, why not take the scenic route? T-237 south to La Grange (Trip 4, this sector) is one of the nicest country rambles in the state. Take time to travel east or west of the highway on the numerous graded county roads. You'll pass gracious old homes, log cabins, churches flanked by tiny cemeteries, and numerous historical landmarks. As you enter Warrenton on T-237 south, watch for a large two-story rock house on the west side of the road. This is the Neece House, built in 1869 and currently being restored as a private residence by its owners. You'll also pass St. Martin's, locally called the smallest Catholic church in the world because it can hold only 12 persons.

From La Grange, follow T-71 southeast to Columbus (Trip 3, this sector) and I-10 east to Houston.

WINEDALE

A 4-mile drive northeast from Round Top on FM-1457 brings you to the Winedale turn-off and another look at yesterday's Texas.

The town is blink-small: a gas station, a combination store and cafe, and a few homes, all tucked into a small valley threaded by Jack's Creek. That old-style split rail fence on the right, however, encircles the most ambitious restoration project in the state, the Winedale Historical Center.

Administered by the University of Texas, this 190-acre outdoor museum covers many pages of the past. The basic farmstead was part of a Mexican land grant to William S. Townsend, one of Austin's second colony. He built a small house on the land about 1834 and in 1848 sold the farm to Samuel Lewis. He in turn expanded the home and the plantation, and by the mid-1850s the Lewis farmhouse was a stage stop on the main road between Brenham and La Grange.

Winedale tours should start at a simple 1855 farm building known as Hazel's Lone Oak Cottage. The next stop is the focal point of the entire museum complex, the Sam Lewis House. This two-story farm house is notable for its authentic Texas primitive furnishings and beautiful wall and ceiling frescoes painted by a local German artist of the time, Rudolph Melchoir. Other rare examples of Melchoir's art can be seen in several of the Henkel Square houses in Round Top.

The Winedale complex has assorted dependencies such as a smokehouse and pioneer kitchen and two other major structures. The old barn, built in 1894 from cedar beams salvaged from an earlier cotton gin, now rings with the ageless words of Shakespeare on August evenings, courtesy of UT English students. Many folks come early and dine from picnic baskets in the pasture.

A 10-minute trek through the back fields leads to the McGregor-Grimm House, a two-story Greek Revival farmhouse built in 1861 and moved to Winedale from Wesley in 1967. As the Lewis House represents the early, rather simple plantation home of the area, the McGregor-Grimm House is gracious and more elaborate, typical of pre-Civil War cotton boom wealth.

The Winedale Historical Center is open only on weekends. Fee. However, the shady grounds and picnic area are open daily at no charge. The Shakespeare performances cost $1, and a reception follows the play. Saturday evening performances traditionally have been preceded by an inexpensive stew dinner served by the staff and cast. 409-278-3530.

WANDERING THE BACKROADS

From Winedale, turn southeast (left) on FM-1457 and go approximately 9 miles to the intersection with T-159. Turn east (left), and it's 19 miles to Bellville — beautiful country all the way.

If you have some time to spare, follow FM-1457 only as far as the tiny town of Shelby and swing north (left) on FM-389. At the intersection with FM-2502, turn right to Wesley. This was an early Czech-Moravian settlement and has the first church of the Czech Brethren faith built in North America (1866). The foundation is original, rock with a huge oak log supporting the center of the building, and the interior has some unusual hand-painted decorations more than a century old.

From Wesley, continue south on FM-2502 to T-159 and turn east (left) to Bellville. If you prefer to explore part of the northwest sector from Wesley, turn north on FM-2502 and then northeast on FM-389 into Brenham (Trip 6, northwest sector). From here, it's US-290 east back to Houston.

BELLVILLE

Settled in 1848 and the Austin County seat, this town on T-159 is named for Thomas Bell, one of Stephen F. Austin's "Old 300," as his first colony has been labeled by history. The best time to visit is during the spring Country Livin' Festival when the routes into the town are lined with bluebonnets and Indian paintbrush. During that festival the chamber of commerce sets up roadside booths where you can get maps and directions to the best flower displays. They also sell packets of bluebonnet seeds so you can sow some of next year's color yourself. For information on Bellville, contact the chamber at P. O. Box 670, Bellville 77418, or call 409-865-3407.

Restoration is bringing back the integrity of the town square. So far, seven buildings have been returned to their original design and color by their owners, and others are soon to be renovated. This has attracted some new boutiques and art galleries, a few of which often are open on Sunday afternoon.

One handsome old home, circa 1906, has been restored by Anna and George Horton into the High Cotton Inn, a cozy Victorian retreat for bed and breakfast. The five guestrooms are furnished in antiques, there's a swimming pool in the garden, and the daily rate includes a bedtime snack at day's end and a plantation breakfast the next morning. The Hortons also serve table d'hote weekend suppers on Friday and Saturday evenings, an outstanding Sunday brunch, and will pack a sack lunch or gourmet picnic for your country trek — if you call in advance. Children are welcome at this grey clapboard mansion, located at 214 South Live Oak, Bellville 77418. 409-865-9796. Watch for it on the west side of T-36 south of town.

Although there are a number of historic markers in town, no vintage homes or buildings are open for tours at this time. One of the local claims to fame is the Bellville Potato Chip Factory, 412 East Main. 409-865-9374. If you've never had a gourmet potato chip, this is the place. Be prepared to pay $.50 for a sampler or $3.95 for a standard bag.

WHERE TO GO

Antique Shops and Art Galleries. For information and a map noting locations of some 20 antique shops and art galleries in town, contact the Bellville Chamber of Commerce at the previously given address.

WHERE TO EAT

Bellville Restaurant. 103 East Main, across from the courthouse. The building dates from 1885, the restaurant from the 1930s. Lunch here is a daily ritual in downtown Bellville. The steam table with its multi-choices of entrees and vegetables is open from 10 a.m. to 1:30 p.m., plus there are daily specials and a regular menu at both lunch and dinner. $-$$. 409-865-9710.

The Hideaway Restaurant. 230 South San Antonio. Chef-owner David Babin is gaining a local following for his Cajun/American offerings, ranging from gumbo and shrimp creole to chicken, steak, and fish dishes. Turn off T-36 south of town at the Jesmar Center (Hellmuth Street) and then turn left on San Antonio to find this modest house-turned-cafe. $-$$. Closed Monday and Tuesday. 409-865-9047.

Los Amigos. One-half block north of the courthouse. Shirley and Joe Sebesta quickly won over Bellville with their killer Margaritas and inventive Tex-Mex food. House specials range from a giant Flour-Rita and shrimp enchiladas to T-bone steaks marinated in their secret sauce. Reservations recommended on weekends. Open daily for lunch and dinner. $-$$. □. 31 N. Bell. 409-865-9745.

The Tea Room & The Tap Room. 17 South Bell, across from the courthouse. It's often standing room only in these connecting establishments. The Tea Room's Tuesday-Saturday lunches are light and tasty, and the Saturday evening dinners are table d'hote, ranging from home-done beef Wellington to pot roast and chicken and dumplings. The Tap Room's Victorian pub atmosphere seems right at home in Bellville. $-$$. 409-865-9720.

WANDERING THE BACKROADS

To return to Houston from Bellville, you again have a choice. FM-529 east is the rural route and intersects T-6 just north of the Bear Creek business area on the northwest side of Houston. If you live in south Houston, your best bet from Bellville is T-36 south 15 miles to Sealy (Trip 1, this sector) where you meet I-10 east for home.

SOUTHWEST

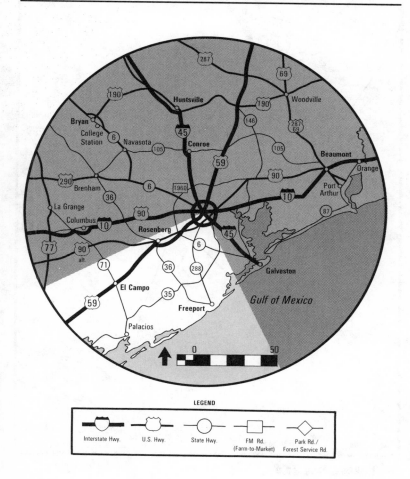

LEGEND

| Interstate Hwy. | U.S. Hwy. | State Hwy. | FM Rd. (Farm-to-Market) | Park Rd./ Forest Service Rd. |

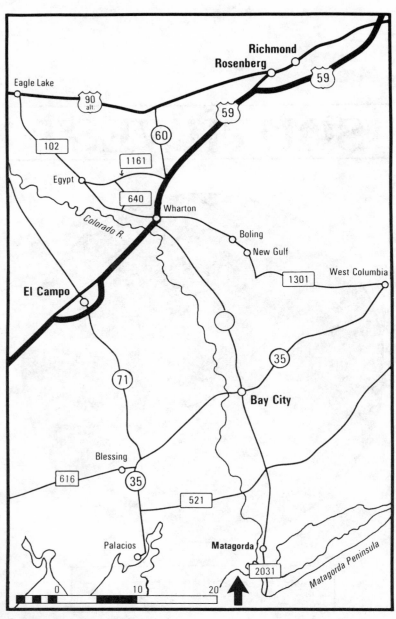

Southwest: Day Trip 1

Day Trip 1

WHARTON
EL CAMPO
PALACIOS
MATAGORDA

WHARTON

This trip through Wharton, El Campo, Palacios, and Matagorda covers a lot of territory, so you may want to consider making a weekend out of it with an overnight at the Luther Hotel in Palacios. Take your fishing and crabbing gear and have fun.

Start your trip via US-59 south to Wharton. While not a gee-whiz destination in itself, Wharton has several pleasures. This rich agricultural land drew Stephen F. Austin's early settlers, and the town of Wharton began about 1846.

Although no homes are open to the public on a regular basis, it's fun to drive down Wharton's oak-shaded streets. Don't miss the old Wharton Home at 219 Burleson or the Prasifca house at 515 Walnut, both private residences, but interesting from the street. Some of the town's old showplaces are open to the public during the Christmas Homes Tour.

Another big celebration in Wharton is the July 4th River Raft Race on the Colorado River — just bring your innertube or homemade raft and jump in, too. For information on these local events as well as a list of the growing number of antique shops, contact the Wharton Chamber of Commerce, 225 Richmond Ave., Wharton 77488. 409-532-1862.

WHERE TO GO

Wharton County Museum. 231 South Fulton, near the river. Some interesting bits and pieces of Wharton's past are gathered here in what was the old jail. While in this neighborhood, take time to mosey around the courthouse and Monterey Square. Donations are appreciated. Closed Monday. 409-532-2600.

Hudgins Goose Hunting. The big sport around Wharton is hunting, available through this family outfit in nearby Hungerford. Even novices are welcome — just bring a shotgun and shells. During the November-through-January hunting season, the Hudgins meet you in Hungerford at 4 a.m., stuff you with breakfast, and then lead you to your specific hunting blind. This is on the central flyway, so you have a good chance of catching your limit of geese. If not, the sunrise in itself is a rare prize. Write P.O. Box 215, Hungerford 77448. 409-532-3198.

The Real McCoy Hunting Club. A club representative meets you, feeds you, and guides you to the hunting area. Hunting available on ponds with duck and geese decoys in each blind or in a variety of fields. Write: P.O. Box 125, Hungerford 77448. 409-532-1370 (weekdays), 409-532-2999 (nights/weekends).

James G. Martin Nuts. 117 South Sunset. This local pecan broker has six mechanical pecan crackers that rarely stop during the harvest months, October through January. You are welcome to stop in and watch. He sells both wholesale and retail, so you can pack some home. Open Monday-Saturday. 409-532-2345.

Cotton Ginning. There are not many places left in Texas to watch a cotton gin do its thing. If you are interested and planning to visit Wharton during the September ginning season, you can visit the Moses Gin through advance arrangement with Caney Valley Cotton Co. Write Box 470, Wharton 77488. 409-532-5210.

WHERE TO EAT

Pier 59. 211 West Elm St. Aside from good prime rib, lobster, salad bar, etc., the big attraction here is the deck overlooking the Colorado River. A great spot to end a day of exploring. $$; □. Closed Sunday and Monday. 409-532-3030.

WANDERING THE BACKROADS

Much of Wharton County sits atop vast sulphur deposits. At the Texas Gulf Sulphur headquarters, 12 miles east of Wharton on FM 1301 between Boling and New Gulf, you can see mountains of the yellow mineral, literally dwarfing nearby railroad cars.

Wharton is surrounded by vast cotton, corn, and rice fields, and the early spring months along any rural road in the area are a fresh vision of green, punctuated by bright wildflowers. Local folks think there is no prettier drive in Texas than FM-102 from Wharton north to Eagle Lake.

This same farm-to-market road takes you through the tiny crossroads town of Egypt, settled by Stephen F. Austin's first colony. Park at the old frame general store and go in for a chat and cool drink. There are nice folks here, plus some fantastic antiques.

Then walk to the old post office with its two vintage gas pumps before looking around the rest of this tiny town. A one-lane road, FM-1161, leads to the Heard-Northington family cemetery and just beyond is the family's old homeplace, Egypt Plantation. Alas, it is open only to groups of 12 or more, but you are welcome to admire this durable pink brick plantation home from the road. It was built in 1849. Egypt

Plantation tours include the Northington-Heard museum, a remarkable collection of Texana housed in the old Egypt-Santa Fe Railroad station depot behind the plantation home. Fee; reservations required. Information: Box 277, Egypt 77436. 409-677-3562.

Another rural drive is along the Spanish Camp Road, FM-640. Watch for the grand Glen Flora Plantation private home on your left, a hint of the Old South.

Nearby, you can have a picnic under 100-year-old pecan trees and pick peaches, nectarines, and Brazos berries at Gundermann's Orchard. Take the Eagle Lake exit from US-59 south and follow FM-102 into Glen Flora. Watch for signs to Gundermann's. 409-677-3319.

EL CAMPO

This spacious town, south on US-59, sits amid a vast coastal grass plain, used for open cattle range from the early 1800s. By the 1850s this area was the starting point for cattle drives across east Texas on the Opelousas and Atascosito trails, heading for the railroad terminals at New Orleans and Mobile.

The railroad eventually made it to this part of Texas, and by the early 1880s the area had an official railroad name, Prairie Switch. Mexican cowboys handling the large herds would camp nearby — thus the name El Campo, which was officially adopted in 1902 when the town was incorporated. Early settlers came from Germany, Sweden, Czechoslovakia, and Ireland, an ethnic mix celebrated on El Campo Grande Day every August.

For information on El Campo, contact the local Chamber of Commerce, Box 446, El Campo 77437. 409-543-2713. The Jackson County Chamber of Commerce has information on Lake Texana and assorted historical sites, 512-782-2382.

WHERE TO GO

Lake Texana. 21 miles southwest of El Campo via US-59. This 11,000 acre lake is noted for its catfish and bass, plus there's good camping and picnicking under shady oaks. All water sports are here, either at the Lake Texana State Park (512-782-5718 or 800-792-1112) or at Lake Texana Marina and Brackenridge Plantation Campground (512-782-7145).

El Campo Museum of Art, Science and History. 201 East Jackson St. The main local attraction is the big game trophy exhibit at this museum. The exhibit was originally in the private collection of a local family. Free. Open daily. 409-543-2714.

WHERE TO EAT

Mikeska's Bar-B-Q. 209 Merchant. Centrally located, this is a favorite spot to pick up some picnic sandwiches or take a road break. $; Open daily. 409-543-5471.

Bob's Place. 114 South Washington. This bakery shows off El Campo's ethnic roots with flavorful kolaches, pigs-in-the-blanket, and cinnamon rolls. $. Closed Sunday. 409-543-9866.

Hillje's Smokehouse. On US-59, four miles west of El Campo. Using an old family recipe, Mike and Betty Jo Prasek turn out memorable smoked sausage and jerky. If you call ahead they'll have a picnic ready to go when you arrive. $-$$; □. Open daily. 512-543-8312.

PALACIOS

When you want to get away from it all, take T-71 south from El Campo to this sleepy fishing community. Whatever you want to leave behind, it isn't here. The big activity for visitors is walking from the Luther Hotel to Peterson's Restaurant, maybe with a short stroll along the bayfront thrown in for excitement.

The area was named Tres Palacios several centuries ago by shipwrecked Spanish sailors who claimed they saw a vision of three palaces on this bay. Unfortunately, the tiny town that began here around the turn of the century doesn't quite live up to its visionary billing. But for day-trippers, it is the perfect low-key escape.

There are two lighted fishing piers, numerous other wood jetties out into the bay, and several public playgrounds and boat ramps. The biggest event of the year is the July 4th Firecracker 200, boat races that attract some of the most powerful hydro racers around.

WHERE TO EAT

Peterson's Restaurant. 420 Main. Almost everything that swims in the Gulf ends up on the table at Peterson's, and the toasted French bread is in a high class by itself. $$; □. Open daily. 512-972-2413.

WHERE TO STAY

The Luther Hotel. On the bay between Fifth and Sixth streets. Quality always lasts, and this rambling white frame hostelry has survived many a storm since its construction in 1903. Sitting with dignity amid a large lawn, this is the kind of place where you watch twilight creep across Palacios Bay while lounging in a chaise on the front porch. Mrs. Luther still runs this Texas Historical Landmark and suggests you have reservations, as she hangs out the "no vacancy" sign with regularity.

The rooms are comfortable, with air conditioning and/or ceiling fans and private baths. There's also a third floor penthouse if you feel like splurging. No food is served in the hotel. Most of the guests congregate around the lobby television set in the evening. 512-972-2313.

WANDERING THE BACKROADS

The main route into Palacios is T-71 south from El Campo. A short turn east on County Road 46 (11 miles south of El Campo) brings you to Danevang Lutheran Church and a memorial to the Danish pioneers who settled here in 1894.

T-71 passes through the outskirts of Blessing. Swing 1 mile west on FM-616 and stop at the old Blessing Hotel, another frame wonder built in 1906 and under restoration. The dining room serves family-style breakfast and lunch, daily. $. Information: P.O. Box 500, Blessing 77419. 512-588-7152.

T-60 is an alternate route to Palacios through neat and orderly Bay City. Take a break at the Matagorda County Museum, 1820 Sixth St., and examine its collection of early Texas maps, carpenter's tools, and other archival material. Open Tuesday-Friday, 3-5 p.m.; Sunday, 2-5 p.m.

If you travel between Palacios and Matagorda, take scenic FM-521. You can't miss Houston Light and Power Company's South Texas Nuclear Plant, under construction on the south side of the road. The free visitor center nearby explains all. Open Monday-Saturday, and Sunday afternoons.

Before you turn south on T-60 to Matagorda, you will see tiny St. Francis Catholic Church and cemetery on the north side of the road. This originally was a Polish village, and the church was rebuilt after the 1895 hurricane swept the settlement away.

MATAGORDA

Founded in 1829, Matagorda, which lies south from Bay City on T-60, thrived as a port and was the third largest town in Texas by 1834. One of the early freight routes that supplied central Texas with the basics of life ran between Matagorda and Austin, with wagons leaving both cities on the 1st and the 15th of every month.

The railroad steamed across Texas by 1853 and bypassed Matagorda in favor of Bay City. A hurricane in 1854 dealt another blow, and Matagorda never regained its early prominence.

Visitors today find a few old churches, a small historical museum in a one-room post office, and a double lock system on the intracoastal canal operated by the U.S. Army Corps of Engineers. One private home is interesting: the Dale-Rugley-Sisk house, built in 1830 at the corner of Catalpa and Fisher streets.

If it's crabbing, seining, or beaching you want, turn south on FM-2031 in the center of town and follow it to the gulf. Along the way are many fine crabbing and fishing holes — just throw in your line where you please. The road literally ends at the beach — 20 miles of it stretching as far as you can see.

Day Trip 2

ANGLETON
BRAZOSPORT
EAST AND WEST COLUMBIA
RICHMOND/ROSENBERG

ANGLETON

Two routes — T-288 and T-35 — come south from Houston and meet in
Angleton before continuing on to the Brazosport area as T-288. You'll
pass the old Brazoria County Courthouse in Angleton, built in 1896 and
expanded in 1916 and again in 1927. One portion of this building now is
the Brazoria County Museum, open Thursday-Saturday, 1-5 P.M., and
well worth a stop. 713-331-6101, ext. 1208.

If you enjoy canoeing, explore Bastrop Bayou, about 5 miles south of
Angleton via both FM-523 and T-288. The best put-in for this 5-mile
float is at the FM-2004 bridge, south of the intersection with FM-523.
The best take-out is 2 miles (by road) further on at the old T-288 bridge
(watch for a railroad track). Even better — float as far as you want and
then turn around and paddle back to your car.

WHERE TO GO

Chenango Orchards. Beginning in mid-May, you can pick all the
peaches and blackberries you want at reasonable cost at this farm near
Rosharon. For information and directions, call 713-431-2138.

BRAZOSPORT

It's hard to find the name Brazosport on current maps, but that's
because it really is nine cities: Brazoria, Freeport, Lake Jackson,
Quintana, Richwood, Surfside, Oyster Creek, Jones Creek, and Clute.

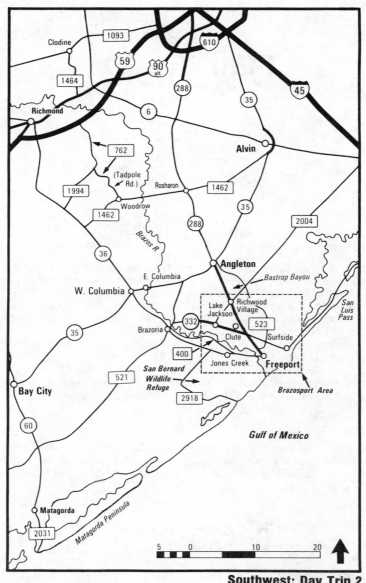

Clodine
1093
59
90 alt.
610
1464
288
35
45
Richmond
6
Alvin
762
(Tadpole Rd.)
1994
Rosharon
1462
35
1462
Woodrow
288
2004
Brazos R.
36
Angleton
E. Columbia
Bastrop Bayou
W. Columbia
Richwood Village
San Luis Pass
Lake Jackson
332
523
35
Clute
Brazoria
Surfside
400
Jones Creek
Freeport
521
San Bernard Wildlife Refuge
Brazosport Area
Bay City
60
2918
Gulf of Mexico
Matagorda
Matagorda Peninsula
2031

5   0   10   20

Southwest: Day Trip 2

Their common bond is the mighty Brazos River as it empties into the Gulf of Mexico.

Actually, the name has its origins on 17th-century nautical charts to mark where the Brazos meets the sea, and Brazosport today is the only mainland community actually on the gulf-front coast of Texas.

This is historic country, but there is little physical evidence left to prove it or provide tourist interest. Without a central community with the architectural charm of old Galveston, the area's biggest draws are the free and unrestricted beaches. Any sunny Sunday finds thousands of cars lined up on the sand, stereos going full blast. Most of the beach-related businesses shut down after Labor Day, and Brazosport reverts to the industrial and refining community it basically is.

There's something going on in some one of the nine towns almost every month of the year. For a schedule of special events as well as information on marinas, vacation rentals, deep sea charter and party boat fishing, etc., contact the Brazosport Tourist Council, Box 2470, Brazosport 77541, or call 409-265-2505. For on-site assistance, visit the Brazosport Chamber of Commerce, 430 West Texas Highway 332, on the frontage road ½ mile west of the T-288 interchange. Open weekdays only.

WHERE TO GO

San Bernard Wildlife Refuge. Ten miles west of Freeport on FM-2918. The best access to this 24,455-acre prairie and marsh preserve is by boat along the Intracoastal Waterway. Established as a quality habitat for wintering migratory waterfowl and other birds, the refuge has recorded more than 400 species of wildlife. There is limited land access for birding, wildlife photography, and general nature observation, but new and improved land facilities are in the planning stages. For on-site assistance, try the maintenance facilities on county road 306, inside the refuge boundaries. Gates always open; no fee. Information: P.O. Drawer 1088, Angleton 77515. 409-849-6062.

Brazosport Center for the Arts and Sciences. On the Brazosport College campus off T-288. This 40,000-square-foot cultural complex is of interest to day visitors primarily for the gem of a natural science museum it contains. Exhibits interpret this coastal region through shells, plants, animals, fossils, minerals, and Indian artifacts. The shell exhibit is particularly well done and will turn your beach trips into expeditions. A new planetarium and cryogenic center have recently been added. Closed Monday. Information: 400 College Drive, Brazosport 77566. 409-265-7831.

The Beaches. The old mouth of the Brazos River becomes, through engineering, the Brazos Harbor Channel and is framed by two jetties ideal for free fishing and crabbing. This channel also divides the beaches. Northeast to San Luis Pass via FM-3005 and the Bluewater Highway (County Road 257) are Surfside and Follet's Island beaches (14 miles of sand). Southwest are Quintana and Bryan Beach State Park (unimproved), reached from T-288 south (Brazosport Boulevard) and County Road 1495.

There is automobile access to all beaches and parking, and camping is where you wish. There are no hook-ups, and public restrooms are extremely limited. Surfside has the most commercial development — rentals, food concessions, etc. If it's solitude you seek, Bryan Beach is your best bet.

Girouard's General Store. 626 West 2nd, Freeport. When *Texas Monthly* magazine labels something the "best" in the state, it's worth a good look. You'll find the wrenches over the bread, plumber's helpers near the pinatas, and nearly everything else tucked somewhere. An outstanding example of a nearly extinct kind of store. If you forgot your crabbing or seining gear, just stop here. Open daily except Sunday. 409-233-4211.

Captain Elliott's Party Boats Inc. 1010 West 2nd, Freeport. In addition to daily deep-sea fishing trips to the snapper banks 30-60 miles off-shore, this firm offers two-hour sightseeing trips on the Old Brazos River on Friday and Saturday evenings. Fee; □. Reservations advised. 409-233-1811.

WHERE TO EAT

Windswept. 105 Burch Circle in Oyster Creek. This is one of the favorite seafood restaurants in the Brazosport area. The house specialties include fresh shrimp dinners and whole flounder. To get here, drive eastbound on T-332 in Surfside, turn left onto FM-523, then right on Linda Lane, right again on Duncan Drive, and right on Burch Circle. The restaurant is behind the Oyster Creek water tower. $$; □. Reservations suggested. Open daily. 409-233-1951.

Cock of the Walk. 920 West 2nd, Freeport. When weather permits, you can eat on the upstairs porch overlooking the river at this early American-style place. Catfish and shrimp are house specialties (you can substitute chicken), along with fried dill pickles, and a good soup/salad/potato bar on the weekday lunch buffet. An oyster bar and ice cream parlours are across the street. $-$$; □. Open daily. 409-233-7715.

The Inn on the Bayou. 5107 Highway 288 (at Bastrop Bayou). This family restaurant is known for its prime rib and variety of fish, including Maryland-style crab cakes. Open for lunch and dinner, Tuesday-Saturday. $-$$; □. 409-265-2297.

WANDERING THE BACKROADS

From Brazosport and environs, this day trip continues via T-36 north to East and West Columbia. Although T-36 is the swiftest route, you also can take the old river road that runs along the Brazos from Jones Creek to Brazoria. To do the latter, start north on T-36 at Freeport, turn east (right) on County Road 400 and continue northwest along the river. At the intersection with FM-521, turn west (left) for about ¾ mile to intersect T-36 and the original routing for this trip.

As you pass through Brazoria, take time to explore. Most of the original town now is flooded by the river, but there are several historical markers worth a stop.

As an alternate to continuing on T-36 to the Columbias, you can follow FM-521 west and T-60 south to Matagorda (Trip 1, this sector).

THE COLUMBIAS — EAST & WEST

As you drive into these two small towns on T-36 and T-35, it's hard to believe they were among the most thriving communities in the state in 1836. East Columbia originally was Bell's Landing, a small port on the Brazos River established in 1824 by one of Austin's first colonists, Josiah H. Bell. Today, East Columbia is almost a ghost town with only a few fine old homes to hint at its early importance.

West Columbia was another enterprise of Josiah Bell. In 1826 he cut a road across the prairie on the west side of the Brazos and created a new town he called Columbia. Within three years it was one of the major trading areas in Texas, and by 1836 some 3,000 people lived here, the rich river bottom land forming the basis for a thriving plantation economy.

After Sam Houston's victory over Santa Anna at San Jacinto, West Columbia came into its own. The most powerful men in Texas came here, designated it the first state capital, created a constitution, and elected Sam Houston the first president of the new republic.

Such glory was short-lived. The town wasn't big enough to house everyone who came to the governmental proceedings, and in 1837 the Legislature met in Houston. But West Columbia had snagged its place in history, and visitors today can visit several interesting sites.

WHERE TO GO

Replica of the First Capitol. On 14th Street, behind the West Columbia Post Office. This successful Bicentennial project recreates the small clapboard building that served as the first capitol of Texas. The original building was a store and survived with a variety of different tenants until its destruction in the violent 1900 storm that devastated much of the Texas coast. The shed room to the right as you enter is thought to have been Stephen F. Austin's office when he served as the first secretary of state for the Republic, and the furnishings of the building, while not original, are antiques from that period. Free. Open Monday-Friday.

The Varner-Hogg State Historic Park. One mile north of T-35 on FM-2852. This land was one of the original land grants from Mexico, part of approximately 4,500 acres given to Martin Varner in 1824. Varner built a small cabin, began running stock, and in 1826 built a rum distillery on his holdings. Stephen F. Austin termed this last enterprise as the first "ardent spirits" made in the Texas colonies. Varner sold his holdings in 1834, and the following year the new owner built a two-story brick house, which survives today. Varner's original cabin is believed to be incorporated into the house, and the bricks, made by slaves, were of material from nearby Brazos riverbed, By the late 1800s this plantation was prospering with sugar cane, cotton, corn and livestock. In 1901 the first native-born governor of Texas, James Hogg, bought the old plantation and regarded the house as the first permanent home his family had. In 1920 the four Hogg children began remodeling the old house. Donated to the state in 1958, it was further restored in 1981. There is a shady picnic area, and guided tours are given whenever a group forms. Closed Monday and Wednesday. Information: P.O. Box 696, West Columbia 77486. 409-345-4656.

Ammon Underwood House. One the river side of Main Street in East Columbia. Built about 1835 and enlarged twice, this stately old home has been surprisingly mobile. It has been moved three times to save it from tumbling into the Brazos. Currently owned and under restoration by the First Capitol Historical Foundation of West Columbia, this is the oldest existing house in the East Columbia community. Many of the furnishings and some of the wallpaper are original, and one room has been left unfinished to show the early construction techniques. A log cabin built prior to 1850 has been moved onto the land behind the Underwood house and is being restored and furnished as a kitchen. Open during the San Jacinto Festival and by appointment. Contact Mrs. Gladys Gupton, 509 Bernard St., West Columbia 77486; 409-345-4213 or the West Columbia Chamber of Commerce. 409-345-3921.

WHERE TO EAT

Columbia Lakes Country Club. 188 Freeman, West Columbia. Although the sporting facilities are for members only, the two dining rooms are open to all. One is formal — no shorts or abbreviated sports clothes please; the second is casual and overlooks the golf course. The weekday lunch buffet and breakfast buffet on weekends are good bets. Open daily for breakfast, lunch and dinner. $-$$; □. 409-345-5151.

RICHMOND/ROSENBERG

Enjoy Richmond while you can. Within a decade it may be swallowed by Houston's urban creep, a historic oasis amid acres of subdivisions. For now, just getting to Richmond and Rosenberg is a pleasure, whether you come north via T-36 from the Columbias or west on US-90A from Houston. The countryside primarily is farms and ranches, shaded by mature pecan trees and a pleasant ride any time of the year.

Richmond literally flows into Rosenberg, the larger of the two towns. Rosenberg was an early shipping site on the Brazos that really boomed when the railroad came to town in 1883. While Rosenberg remains the commercial center, the two towns have shared a common history for the past century. A strong Czech population leads to the annual Czech Fest on the first weekend of May at the Fort Bend County Fairgrounds. The county fair again livens things up around the first of October. For day-trippers, Richmond is the more historically interesting of the two towns.

In Texas time Richmond is very old, one of the first permanent settlements of Stephen F. Austin's original 300 colonists. For centuries the Brazos River had made a big bend here, each flood leaving more rich soil in its wake. Shortly after Christmas Day, 1821, five men staked their fortunes on this fertile land, building a two-room fort just below the bend, thus the name Fort Bend County. Today a marker stands on this site, between the eastbound and westbound bridges of US-90A as it crosses the Brazos.

The settlement thrived with the addition of Thompson's ferry, northwest in the bend of the river, and in 1837 the townsite of Richmond was formally laid out on the site of the old fort. By 1843 a sugar mill was in operation at nearby Sugar Land, the forerunner of today's Imperial Sugar plant, and sugar cane plantations were thriving throughout the area by the 1860s.

Richmond had some now-famous residents, among them Mirabeau Lamar, Deaf Smith, and Jane Long. Carrie Nation ran a hotel on the corner of Fourth and Morton streets before she took up the battle against demon rum.

Visitors today find several reminders of Richmond's colonial past, but the overriding feeling is that of exploring small-town America, circa 1920. Somehow it is reassuring to discover a corner drug store and a five and dime within the shadow of an old-fashioned courthouse. A walk along Richmond's main drag, Morton Street, is an architectural antidote to Houston's skyscrapers.

A detailed map walks you along the oak-shaded streets to all the local historic sites, courtesy of the Fort Bend County Museum. They are available at the museum or from the Richmond-Rosenberg Chamber of Commerce, 4120 Avenue H, Rosenberg 77471. Call 713-342-5464.

WHERE TO GO

The Fort Bend County Courthouse. Fourth and Jackson streets. This fifth courthouse was built with an air of majesty in 1908 and so well refurbished in 1981 that it was cited by the Houston chapter of the American Institute of Architects. It also is the one and only building in Fort Bend County listed in the National Register of Historic Places. More notable features are the three-story rotunda, the mosaic tile floors, and the rich woodwork on the stairs and in the main courtroom. Free. Open Monday-Friday.

Fort Bend County Museum. Fifth and Houston streets. Just about every aspect of area history is covered here with displays including items or manuscripts of Lamar, Carrie Nation, Jane Long, and others. One diorama tells the harrowing tale of early railroad crossings on the Brazos, and a special exhibit room has a changing show of assorted archive and reserve materials.

The museum staff also gives demonstrations of frontier skills and will guide historical tours of Richmond by advance notice. Closed Monday. Free. Information: P.O. Box 251, Richmond 77469. 713-342-6478.

John H. Moore House. Fifth and Liberty streets. Built in 1883 on the present museum grounds, this gracious old home looks as though it will stand for several more centuries. It now is a museum in itself, notable for its slave-cut picket fence and turn-of-the-century furnishings. Fee. Guided tours on Sunday only 1-5 p.m.

Decker Park. North of the railroad tracks at Sixth and Preston streets. Three buildings moved here mark the beginning of a living history museum: a 1902 railroad depot, a log cabin replica of the 1822 fort, and the 1850s McNabb House, once owned by Carrie Nation's daughter. The Victorian brick relic across Preston Avenue was the county jail from 1896 to 1948 and now houses the Confederate Museum. The South may rise again — the collection includes muskets, rifles, guns, uniforms, pictures, money, letters, and other memorabilia relating to the Civil War. Free. Open Sunday 2-4 P.M.

Imperial Sugar Co. 198 Kempner, Sugar Land. From US-90A, turn north on Kempner and park where you find space. On the site of the S.M. Williams cane plantation established in the 1840s, this modern plant gives visitors a look at sugar from the raw product to final packaging. The free tours are interesting, and reservations are not necessary except for groups. Tours are given Monday-Friday. For information write P.O. Box 9, Sugar Land 77478. 713-491-9181.

Arroyo Seco Historical Park. Southeast on FM-762. Due to open soon, this park is a project of the privately funded George Foundation. Route 1, Box 177, Richmond 77469. 713-343-0415. (See Wandering the Backroads, this section.)

WHERE TO EAT

The Brass Whale. 101 Liberty at the eastbound US-90A bridge in Richmond. This family-run restaurant specializes in absolutely fresh seafood, right down to the homemade gumbo. $$; □. Closed Monday. 713-342-7858.

Liberty Street Tea Room and Gift Gallery. 315 Liberty St., Richmond. Julie Lee whips up some outstanding daily specials plus fresh croissant sandwiches, five kinds of salad in two sizes, assorted quiches, etc. If you've never sampled a breakfast taco, this is the place. Open Monday-Saturday for breakfast and lunch. $; □. Reservations suggested. 713-342-7015.

WANDERING THE BACKROADS

An alternate route from Houston to Richmond forsakes US-59 and US-90A and instead rambles west out Westheimer (FM-1093) past its intersection with T-6. At Clodine, turn south on FM-1464 for about 10 miles and then west (right) on US-90A into Richmond.

Another country ramble takes the long way home. From Richmond, turn south on FM-762 (Eleventh Street/Thompson Road) and follow its zigzag southeasterly course through the countryside. Just beyond Crabb, FM-762 turns further south as the A.P. George Road (sign also will read FM-1994). Stay on FM-762 as it jogs onto Tadpole Road. At the intersection with FM-1462 at Woodrow, turn east (left) to intersect T-288 and then north (left) toward home and Houston.

This FM-762 route has several surprises and it's worth remembering for the future. First are the wonderful old homes being restored as part of the Arroyo Seco Historical Park, a project of the privately funded George Foundation. The site is the historic Jones family cemetery and the A.P. George Ranch, and the buildings have been moved here from other locations where they were endangered.

The restoration is being done with care and ultimately will serve as a base for information about the entire Fort Bend County and Gulf Coast region. For now, please admire only from the road. Those "no trespassing" signs mean business, and the staff strongly discourages drop-in visitors.

Farther along the Tadpole Road section of FM-762, the new Brazos Bend State Park is a delight along Big Creek, a tributary of the Brazos. The facilities include screened shelters, trailer sites with water and electricity, tent sites with water, and primitive sites with no water that require a hike in. Almost all are shaded with massive oaks. In addition to two fishing piers where you can angle for bass, catfish or crappie, there are hiking and nature trails, seven photography platforms for shooting the park's exceptional wildlife, and an interpretive center. For information, call 800-792-1112 or 409-553-3243.

NORTHEAST

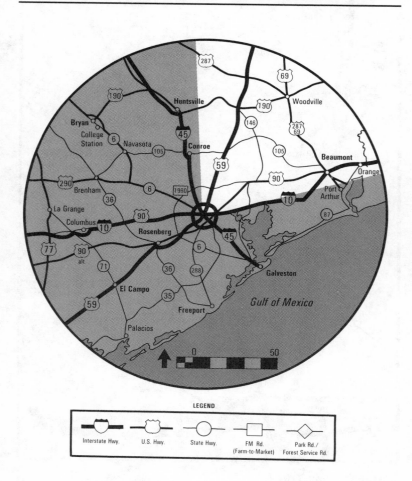

LEGEND

| Interstate Hwy. | U.S. Hwy. | State Hwy. | FM Rd. (Farm-to-Market) | Park Rd. / Forest Service Rd. |

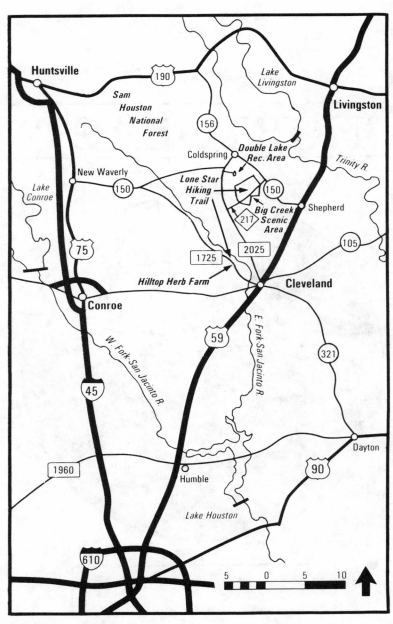

Northeast: Day Trip 1

Day Trip 1

HUMBLE
CLEVELAND
COLDSPRING

HUMBLE

Like the small town of Spring in north Harris County, there are two Humbles — old and new. The new is easy to find, a bright forest of franchise signs and shopping centers around the US-59 north/FM-1960 interchange. Old Humble lies quietly behind, east of the railroad tracks and south of FM-1960.

Back in 1865 a fisherman named Pleasant Smith Humble established a small ferry across the San Jacinto River near where US-59 crosses it today. Things remained quiet until the railroad came to town about 1878, and Humble became a flag stop on the narrow-gauge HE & WT line, running between Houston and Shepherd. Settlers came, and by 1886 it was officially a town.

Rich with timber, Humble fed a growing logging industry. Back in 1887 a local lumberman, Jim H. Slaughter, rafted logs down the San Jacinto for milling. Pulling into a small backwater to make an overnight camp, he noticed bubbles seeping along the river bank. When his match brought a flame, he rightly concluded the presence of natural gas and subsequently bought 60 acres of land in the area. Although he personally didn't profit greatly, this was the beginning of the first oil field in Humble and Harris County.

The first wells came into production in 1904, and by mid-1905 the field was producing more barrels per day than any other in the state. Humble got busy earning the reputation as one of the toughest towns in Texas. The Moonshine Hill area east of town soon had a population of 25,000, and Texas Rangers often had to be called on to keep some semblance of law and order.

In 1909 the Humble Oil and Refining Co. was formed in a small tin-roofed building on Humble's Main Street, one of its organizers being the local feed store owner, Ross Sterling. The company was successful and ultimately became the Exxon we know today. Sterling didn't do too badly either. Previously the owner of a chain of feed stores, he soon bought the Humble State Bank and carved a niche in the state's history as a newspaper publisher, oilman, and governor of Texas from 1931 to 1933.

As quickly as it came, the oil boom disappeared — no new wells were coming in — and by 1915 Humble once again was a small, quiet community strongly dependent on lumber and agriculture for its financial base. Then a second oil strike at greater depth in 1929 brought new life, and Humble was chartered as a city in 1933. Visitors today can tour the still-working oil field (look for the Moonshine Hill Loop sign 2 miles east of town on FM-1960). This stretch of road between Humble and Moonshine Hill was the first concrete road in Harris County.

Humble's Main Street now is a stroll through small-town Americana. Antique stores, galleries, and other less glamorous small businesses are thriving here because rents are relatively low. A renewed interest in preserving what has survived from Humble's past keeps things moderately spiffed up. Stop for a moment at the corner of FM-1960 and North Houston Avenue and see the oldest artesian well in the area, drilled as a wildcat oil venture in 1912.

WHERE TO GO

Humble Historical Museum. 110 West Main St., next to City Hall. One happy grass-roots result of America's Bicentennial celebration, this small museum is bursting with a collection of old things donated by local residents. Free, but donations are appreciated. Closed Monday and Wednesday. 713-446-9881.

Mercer Arboretum. 22306 Aldine-Westfield Rd., Humble. This 214-acre county park is a sleeper, often overlooked by day-trippers. What they miss is an outstanding collection of native Texas plants, nature trails, a bird sanctuary, fern garden, picnic areas, and Indian information, all along a wooded stretch of Cypress Creek. Coming soon: eight-mile canoe floats from Spring Creek to Jesse Jones Park, a $500,000 information and education center, wildflower habitat, and children's play area. 1.25 miles north of FM-1960. Free; open daily except major holidays. 713-443-8731.

Survival Games of Texas. Capture the flag game for adults, played in the wild woods between New Caney and Splendora. Weekends only; reservations required. Fee. 409-955-6696.

WHERE TO EAT

Edelweiss. 503 North Main St. One of the nicest refurbishings in town, this substantial old home is the spot for good food with strong Austrian-German-Swiss accents, with wines to match. House specialties include wiener schnitzel, veal Zurich, and smoked pork loin, and the daily specials result from what the chef found fresh and best at market. Children are welcome, and reservations are advised for dinner. $$; □. Closed Sunday. 713-540-1003.

Chez Nous. 217 South Avenue G, South Humble. In addition to a menu that features many of the French classics, chef/owner Gerard Brach creates outstanding daily specials such as fresh Dover sole or fresh swordfish in an avocado/lime butter. French-born and trained, he taught a wine course at Four Seasons in NYC, expertise that shows on Chez Nous' wine list. A jewel of a restaurant in an unlikely setting, a 100-year old church, Chez Nous is worth a day-trip in itself. $$-$$$; □. Open Monday through Saturday for dinner; reservations advised. Ask directions. 713-446-6717.

WANDERING THE BACKROADS

For a taste of woods and lake, consider renting a canoe (with livery) from Outdoor Adventures and floating the east fork of the San Jacinto River above Lake Houston. From Humble, continue north on US-59 and turn east on FM-1485 in New Caney. Information: 713-689-5457.

CLEVELAND

Back in the 1880s this railroad town on US-59 north of Houston thrived with lumber shipping. Now it is better known as a major gateway to the forest and water wonderland that covers most of San Jacinto County and as the home of the Hilltop Herb Farm.

WHERE TO GO

Big Creek Scenic Area. This 1,130-acre preserve has numerous hiking trails, wild and varied topography, spring-fed creeks, and abundant wildlife. Part of the 350,000-acre Big Thicket that spatters across vast portions of southeast Texas, Big Creek claims the state champion magnolia tree. The Lone Star Hiking Trail begins near Montague Church on FM-1725 and loops through the scenic area. From Cleveland, continue north on US-59 12 miles to Shepherd, then west on T-150 for 6 miles to Forest Service Road 217. Information: San Jacinto District Office, Sam Houston National Forest, 407 North Belcher, Cleveland 77327; 713-592-6462.

Double Lake Recreation Area. FM-2025, 15 miles north of Cleveland. This 25-acre lake is edged by picnic and camping areas and has a beach and bathhouse with showers. No motor boats are allowed, but canoeing is popular. Information: use address and telephone number for Big Creek Scenic Area listed above.

WHERE TO EAT

Hilltop Herb Farm. Ten and a half miles northwest of Cleveland on FM-1725. Back in 1957 when Madalene and Jim Hill decided to retire to their farm in the Sam Houston National Forest and grow herbs, they found instead a hobby of life-changing dimensions. Growing herbs led to outside sales and then to the establishment of the Garden Room where memorable table d'hote meals are served. Each meal is planned around an entree, fresh vegetables, and fruits, all seasoned with a variety of fresh herbs.

Aided by their daughter and her family, Mrs. Hill tours her guests through the herb gardens and greenhouses, giving a running commentary on what's what, how it is used, and any curious niche it might occupy in history. The new Garden Room offers dining amid ferns, vines, and baskets of fragrant flowers and herbs, and a small shop called the Gallimaufrey sells condiments, jams, herbs, and sauces. Tasting is encouraged before you buy.

No meals are served from July 15 to Aug. 31 or from Dec. 15 to Feb. 28, and there is no tipping or smoking. There is no tipping because they don't consider themselves a restaurant, and the no-smoking policy is explained in their brochure. It states that "cancer will probably kill the smokers, but we can't wait that long; the soup will be cold."

Meal reservations are required three to six weeks in advance, and cancellations are honored only if made 30 days prior to your lunch or dinner date. $$$; □. Call for hours: 713-592-5859. The farm is open to visitors Monday-Saturday, with no reservations needed. For information write P.O. Box 1734, Cleveland 77327.

Dolly's Ice Cream Parlour. 1206 Houston St. (From US-59 turn east at the second traffic light in Cleveland [T-321] and go 1 mile to the Hillcrest Center.) Ever had a fried ice cream? If not, don't leave Cleveland without one. Here you'll get scoops of Blue Bell ice cream coated with the owner's own mix of cinnamon and spices. The ice cream is flash fried in oil and served up in a dainty dish with assorted toppings. The coating mix is also sold on the premises, and if you want to try frying ice cream yourself, recipes are included in the price. This neat-as-a-pin pastel parlour and bakery also serves quiche, soups, sandwiches, pies, and cakes to eat there or to go. $. 713-592-0297.

Boyett's Restaurant. 1002 South Washington (US-59). Home-cooked Texas standards are the rule here, and the cinnamon rolls were named the best in the state by *Texas Monthly*. Open daily. $-$$; □. 713-592-2601.

WANDERING THE BACKROADS

T-150 between Shepherd and Coldspring cuts through a corner of the Sam Houston National Forest.

An 8-mile jaunt southeast of Cleveland on T-321 toward Dayton will bring you to Well's Store, formerly the gathering place for the Tarkington Prairie community and a stage stop on the old Lynchburg-Nacogdoches Road. The center portion of this old mercantile store was built in 1875, and the grounds are used for an antique fair in the spring.

COLDSPRING

This old community was called Coonskin when it was founded in 1847. Now the San Jacinto county seat, it's beginning to be a tourist center. The fourth Saturday of every month is a popular Trades Day, selling everything from antiques to food. You'll find a small but interesting museum in the old jail, open weekend afternoons, plus there are numerous historical markers around town. The United Methodist Church was built in 1848 and the old brick jail in the 1880s.

Getting to Coldspring is a day-tripper's delight. From Cleveland, take FM-2025 north for 17 miles, then turn east on T-150 another 2 miles. This takes you through a major portion of the Sam Houston National Forest. An alternate route leaves US-59 north at Shepherd and follows T-150 west 11 miles to Coldspring.

WHERE TO EAT

County Seat Restaurant. One block from courthouse square at the end of Slade St. This country place specializes in fried catfish, but the steaks, salad bar, fried chicken and other goodies are tasty also. This old home is filled with antiques and sited on beautiful grounds edged with live oaks and some of the natural spring-fed streams that give Coldspring its name. Open Thursday-Sunday. $-$$; □. 409-653-4001.

WANDERING THE BACKROADS

If you want to visit the Lake Livingston area (Trip 2, this sector), take T-156 north from Coldspring to its intersection with US-190 and turn east. From Livingston, take US-59 south to home.

An alternate is to drive west from Coldspring on T-150 to New Waverly and I-45. A turn north (right) on I-45 takes you to Huntsville and Madisonville (Trip 2, northwest sector). From there, it's south on I-45 to home.

Day Trip 2

LIVINGSTON
WOODVILLE

LIVINGSTON

Due to a fire that wiped out three downtown blocks around the turn of the century, little is left of Livingston's beginnings back in 1846. Today, this timber town is 76 miles north of the heart of Houston via US-59. The seat of Polk County, it is important to day-trippers in several ways.

Every fall, the forest around Livingston looks like the rolling hills of western Massachusetts when the frosts bring up the color in the maples, sassafras, oak, sweet gum, sumac, and hickory. One of the town's biggest attractions is 90,000-acre Lake Livingston, 15 miles west of downtown. The lake primarily is an impoundment of the Trinity River, and there are three short but beautiful river float trips possible below the dam. Access is at the dam, at the US-59 crossing south of Livingston, and at FM-105 near Romayor. The final take-out is at the FM-162 crossing east of Cleveland.

All of Polk County is crossed with old Indian traces, the remains of which are noted on highway signs. No trails are still in existence, but each is marked in several places.

For information on Lake Livingston or the general area, contact the Polk County Chamber of Commerce, 516 West Church, Livingston 77351. 409-327-4929.

WHERE TO GO

Polk County Museum. 601 West Church in the Murphy Memorial Library. Exhibits from the early days of Polk County, plus some interesting Indian artifacts. Note the old Jonas Davis log cabin across the street. Donation. Open Monday-Friday. 409-327-8192.

Lake Livingston. There is good public access through Lake Livingston State Park. Facilities include a swimming pool, paddle and boat rental, an activity center, hiking and biking trails, picnic areas, campsites, and screened shelters.

From Livingston, take US-59 south 2.5 miles and turn west on

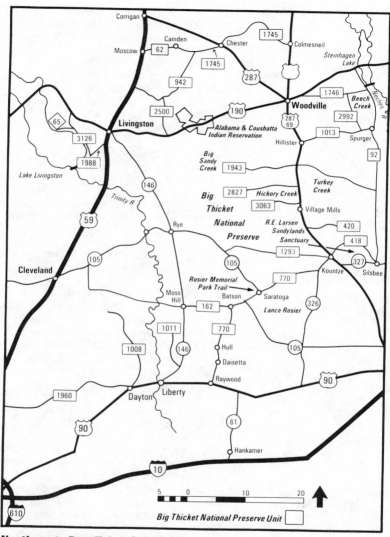

Northeast: Day Trips 2 and 3

FM-1988, then north on FM-3126 to Park Road 65. There are numerous private resorts, marinas, and campgrounds along this route where you can arrange fishing guides or rent boats. Information: Route 9, Box 1300, Livingston 77351. 409-365-2202.

Colquitt's Syrup Mill. From Livingston, continue north on US-59 9 miles and turn east on FM-942 for approximately 15 miles. Turn right on a dirt road just before Beard's Cemetery and swing right again at the first fork to find one of the few old-fashioned sugar cane mills left in east Texas. Just stop at the first house on your left and knock on the door. Mr. and Mrs. Colquitt, the owners, will be glad to show you the small mill out back.

The crushers in this old mill are more than 100 years old and going strong, driven by belt from a tractor motor. The juice is sluiced off into long open pans and boiled down into syrup, a simple, time-honored process.

The crushing season starts about the second week in November and lasts as long as the cane does or until a hard freeze hits. The mill often runs full-tilt seven days a week until Christmas, so November and December are prime times to visit here. You are welcome to watch, sample a bit, and maybe even buy some cans of the moderately priced light and tasty syrup. Some folks come just to buy the raw juice to make their own home brew.

The rest of the year the mill is abandoned to the weeds and elements, and there isn't much to see, although the Colquitts sell syrup until there isn't any left. If you want to check on that syrup supply or make sure the mill is in operation, give them a call at 409-563-2340.

Alabama-Coushatta Indian Reservation. On US-190, 17 miles east of Livingston. This 4,600-acre reservation in the Big Thicket is self-supporting, thanks to a well-executed camping-recreation-tourist complex. Start at the museum for some historical background and then tour the Big Thicket forest, by either miniature railroad or swamp buggy. Except for a trail, this is the only public access to the Big Sandy Creek unit of the Big Thicket National Preserve. More than 100 species of trees are native to this reservation, including eight varieties of oak, the state champion water hickory and laurel oak trees, and a huge 200-year-old magnolia. The tours go through virgin forest, and you may surprise an alligator or two in the swamp regions. Fee.

Also located here is an Indian village replica where tribal members demonstrate early housing, crafts, and foods. Tribal dances representing war, courtship, harvest, and tribute are performed in an adjacent area. Admission fee.

The Alabama-Coushatta Indians are famed for their baskets, hand-woven from the rare long-leaf pine. Many have lids and are shaped like animals, and all are considered collector's items. A few usually are for sale in the village store, and some rare oldies are displayed in the Polk County Museum in Livingston.

An open-air historical pageant keeps things lively on summer nights. *Beyond the Sundown* dramatizes the Alabama-Coushattas' attempt to remain neutral during Texas' struggle to gain independence from Mexico. The curtain goes up Monday through Saturday at 8:30 p.m., June-August. Fee. 409-563-4777.

Slightly removed from the central complex is 25-acre Lake Tombigbee, site for camping, picnicking, and swimming. Canoeing and fishing for bass, perch, and catfish also are popular.

The reservation is closed December-February, on Monday and Tuesday during March and November, and on Monday during April and October. The hours of operation also vary, so inquire before you come. Information: Route 3, Box 640B, Livingston 77351. 409-563-4391.

Johnson's Rock Shop. Ten miles east of Livingston off US-190 in the Indian Springs Lake Estates. Stop at the Texaco gas and grocery store, and call for directions to this lapidary. You'll see more than 1.5 million pounds of rock, and just about that many varieties, plus the equipment used to cut, polish, and finish it. Visitors are welcome, and there's no fee for a personal tour. Open daily. 409-563-4438.

WHERE TO EAT

White Kitchen Cafe. 417 Washington (US-59), one block north of the US-190 intersection. Standard Texas tummy-filling fare, topped off with homemade pies warm from the oven. $-$$; □. Open daily. 409-327-4716.

Dandy Donuts. 913 Washington (US-59). Folks drive for miles to snack on these sinfully good sinkers, as well as cookies, brownies, and kolaches. $. Open daily. 409-327-9120.

Rachal Brothers Seafood Market and Restaurant. Two miles west of US-59 on TX 190. Pronounced Ra-Shall, this tiny and simple restaurant specializes in seafood prepared Cajun-style. Manny and Gene Rachal are from Lafayette, La., and serve a mean etouffe, boiled and fried shrimp, raw and fried oysters, and seafood gumbo. Open Monday-Saturday, $-$$. 409-967-0100.

WOODVILLE

Woodville is located 33 miles northeast from Livingston via US 190. Although history has been relatively quiet here, the town has some surprises in store for those who take the time to poke around. Not only are there 21 historical markers in the area, the entire town is a bird sanctuary and serves as the northern gateway to the Big Thicket.

Founded between 1846 and 1847 as the county seat for newly created Tyler County, Woodville is aptly named, surrounded by miles of rolling forest. The best times to go are late March and early April when the Tyler County Dogwood Festival stirs things up a bit, or in the fall after the first cold snap coats the woods with some of the prettiest colors in the state. Brochures and maps are available from the Tyler County Chamber of Commerce, 507 North Pine St. Woodville 75979. 409-283-2632.

In the heart of town is the courthouse, a distinctive architectural piece when it was built in 1891 for the munificent sum of $21,609. A 1930s remodeling stole its baroque charm and reduced it to mundane and functional.

WHERE TO GO

James Edward Wheat House. At the corner of Charlton and Wheat streets. One portion of this home was built in 1848. It is a private residence, but you are welcome to enjoy the exterior.

Alan Shivers Library and Museum. Two blocks north of the courthouse at 303 North Charlton. The late Governor Alan Shivers has his roots in Woodville, and this restored Victorian showplace houses his papers and memorabilia of the Shivers family and the town. Fee. Open Monday-Saturday, Sunday by appointment. 409-283-3709.

Heritage Garden Village. One mile west of US-190. You can't miss this place — just look for a giant wood clock with a mouse on the side, the creation of owner Clyde E. Gray. This is the piece de resistance of what Gray calls the only see-and-touch museum town in America. In addition to the clock, visitors can prowl a rambling conglomeration of Americana which includes the world's only flying outhouse, old log cabins, and an old-time newspaper plant.

The works of the aforementioned clock were built by Seth Thomas in 1902 and for many years graced the Houston City Hall on Old Market Square. Removed from its original housing in 1940 and then stored, it ended up in a junk yard where Clyde Gray bought it. He restored the works to running condition and then successfully fought off court demands by Houston history buffs that it be returned to the city. Open daily, 9 a.m.-sundown. Fee. Information: P.O. Box 666, Woodville 75979. 409-283-2272. (Note: the Pickett House Restaurant is here also; see following description.)

Dogwood Trail. This 1.5-mile walking trail along Theuvenin Creek is maintained by the International Paper Company. Watch for their sign 3 miles east of Woodville on US-190.

Texas Rockers. Southwest of Woodville on Cobb Mill Road. Hugh and Jennie Vaughn's beautiful hardwood rockers grace the governor's office and homes of assorted celebrities. Visitors are welcome to watch them being made, but call ahead to be sure the Vaughns are not away exhibiting. Closed Sunday. □. 409-283-5627.

Martin Dies Jr. State Park. On Steinhagen Lake, 14 miles east of Woodville on US-190. The usual water/lake activities such as fishing, picnicking, and camping are here. For information, write Route 4, Box 274, Jasper 75951, or call 409-384-5231.

River Floating. Steinhagen Lake, east on US-190, also is known as Dam B, an impounding of the Neches River. If you are interested in floating the Neches below the dam, call the U.S. Army Corps of

Engineers office at Steinhagen Lake (409-429-3491) for a report on conditions and whether the river is floatable.

Lake Tejas. Eleven miles north of Woodville via US-69, then east one mile on FM-256. When summer's heat hits, this super swimming hole is the place to be. Operated on May weekends and daily by the local school district June through Labor Day, this sand-bottom lake has a two-level dive platform, sundecks over the water, lifeguards, bathhouse, and both picnicking and camping (year round). Fee. 409-837-5201 or 409-837-2225 weekdays.

Big Thicket Information: The north district office of the Big Thicket National Preserve is at 507 North Pine at Woodville. Open Monday-Friday. 409-283-5824.

Jones Country Music Park. On Route 255 near Colmesneil. Some of the best of live country music from Merle Haggard, Mel Tillis, and Willie Nelson to local performers play this giant outdoor stage weekends from April through October. Reservations also accepted for the RV park. Store, playground, and picnic tables on-site. For camping, program, and ticket information, call 409-837-5463 or write P.O. Box 730, Ducette 75942.

WHERE TO EAT

Pickett House. One mile west on US-190, behind Heritage Garden Village. This old school house has been converted into an all-you-can-stuff-in kind of place, with bright circus posters on the walls and chicken and dumplings in the pot. The menu also includes a second entree, usually fried chicken or locally caught fish — but no hamburgers, steaks, etc. These boarding house-style meals also include your choice of fresh buttermilk, milk, or real made-from-scratch ice tea; three vegetables; tomato pickles; watermelon rind preserves; cornbread; and fruit cobbler. A special fried catfish dinner is served on Fridays. It's fetch your own drinks and then take your dirty dishes to the kitchen, just like home. $$. Open daily. 409-283-3946.

The Homestead Restaurant. In Hillister. Take US-69/287 south 8 miles from Woodville, turn east for one block on FM-1013, and then right just before the railroad tracks. Not to worry — there are some signs, and this restaurant is worth searching for. Two refugees from Houston, Emily and Otho Sumner, offer country dining with a gourmet touch in a marvelous old home they have restored. Built around 1912 in nearby Hillister, the house was moved by the Sumners to its present 13-acre shady site and fixed up with charm, including swings on the porch. In addition to some nice touches on the standard fish/steak/chicken offerings, there are two nightly specials; lunches run to inventive salads and sandwiches. They make their own salad dressings, and because Emily Sumner is a pie freak, the cook goes crazy with desserts. Tough choices might include Japanese fruit pie, fresh peach icebox pie, or a pecan and Philadelphia cream cheese creation called the Homestead Delight.

Local artists' work is displayed in the main hall, proving there's lots of talent in these piney woods. Reservations are strongly advised. No liquor is served, but chilled wine glasses are provided. $$. Open Thursday-Sunday. 409-283-7324 or 409-283-7244.

WANDERING THE BACKROADS

From Woodville, then 1.3 miles drive northwest on US-287 to Chester north on FM-1745 to see John Henry Kirby's community meeting house and chapel. Follow the signs in town to Peachtree Village. Built in 1912 as a community hall by lumber magnate John Henry Kirby, it is under restoration by the Tyler County Historical Society. If it isn't open and you want to see inside, ask at the caretaker's house.

Another scenic drive takes you from Woodville to Saratoga (Trip 3, this sector). Take US-69/287 south from Woodville to Kountze, swing southwest on T-326, and turn right on FM-770 to Saratoga and the heart of Big Thicket country. To continue home to Houston, follow FM-770 south to US-90 and turn west.

If you need a swifter return home from Woodville, retrace your route back to Livingston via US-190 and turn south on US-59.

Day Trip 3

LIBERTY-DAYTON
BIG THICKET

(See map, p. 101)

LIBERTY-DAYTON

Although this area, east of Houston on US-90, is rich with history, much of what survives remains privately owned, and the towns have little to illustrate their heritages. Take away the historical markers, and the casual tourist might conclude that nothing much has happened here — which is far from the truth.

Originally, this entire corner of Southeast Texas was called the Atascosito District, a municipality first of Spain and then of Mexico. Now broken into ten counties, the early focus of the district was the outpost of Atascosito, shown as a fresh-water spring on maps as early as 1757. To reach the original site of Atascosito today, take T-146 northeast from Liberty approximately 4 miles and turn west (left) on FM-1011. A marker is just beyond the intersection, and the spring still flows nearby.

After 1821 this wilderness was controlled by Mexico, which welcomed Anglo settlers. For the most part those early settlers were independent individuals who came here because they could not gain grants through Austin's colonization farther to the west. They formed settlements like Liberty and Dayton, and many other places whose names have faded from map and memory.

The Atascosito Road crossed the district, running from Goliad and Refugio to Opelousas, Louisiana. Today its route is roughly paralleled by US-90, and the town of Dayton straddles the historic path.

In 1831, Villa de la Santissima Trinidad de la Libertad was established slightly south of the spring, officially laid out with six public squares. Now called Liberty, it traditionally is considered to be the third-oldest town in Texas.

Two maps available from the chamber of commerce will direct you to most of the sites of interest, including St. Stephen's Episcopal Church (1898), 2041 Trinity; the Cleveland-Partlow Home (1860), 2131 Grand (private); and the T.J. Chambers Home (1861), 624 Milam (private).

Graveyard historians will love Liberty — there are at least four historic cemeteries in the area. For information write the Liberty-Dayton Chamber of Commerce, Box 1270, Liberty 77575 or call 409-336-5736.

Six miles west on US-90 and across the Trinity River is Dayton. Originally, it was called West Liberty and then Day's Town in honor of an early settler, I.C. Day. At first a lumber and agricultural community, Dayton later was boosted financially by the coming of the railroad in the 1870s and again by oil in the early 1920s. Passing through, take time to read the historical marker concerning the Runaway Scrape (Trip 3, west sector). This marker is on the eastern outskirts of Dayton on US-90 east.

WHERE TO GO

Old French Cemetery. Approximately 3 miles east of Dayton on FM-1008. Established in 1830, this is the burial place of some of the early settlers of the Atascosito district. One grave notes an 1821 death, and others are enclosed inside an antique iron fence.

Geraldine Humphreys Cultural Center. 1710 Sam Houston St., Liberty. Local and pioneer history plus special art exhibits are here. An active little theatre, the Valley Players, puts on plays and musicals here at various times. For current playbill, call 409-336-5887. A contemporary bell tower houses an exact replica of the famous Liberty Bell, cast in 1960 by a London foundry from the original pattern and mold. The bell rings twice a year — on New Year's Day and again on the Fourth of July during an old-fashioned Independence Day celebration on the center grounds. Free. Open Monday-Saturday. 409-336-8901. (Liberty library).

Sam Houston Regional Library and Research Center. Four miles north of Liberty via T-146 and a turn northwest (left) on FM-1011. This massive repository is a double surprise. First, it has three public display rooms full of goodies like Jean Lafitte's personal diary and other remnants of the days when Liberty was a major steamboat port on the Trinity River. Second, it is sited very near the original settlement of Atascosito on a high knoll graced with mature pecan trees.

This library has reprints of one of the earliest censuses taken in Texas, the Atascosito Census of 1826, prized by genealogists because it lists the maiden names of wives.

Currently undergoing restoration on the museum grounds is the historic Gillard-Duncan Home. Built about 1848 in Ames, an early Creole community south of Liberty, the house is shown by appointment. Perhaps more historic restorations will nestle under these pecan trees in the future, a perfect counterpoint to the sleek research center in both architecture and theme. The library-research center is owned by the state and operated by the Texas State Library. Within its fireproof preservation vaults are valuable historic records, documents, portraits, and other artifacts of the original Atascosito district. Free. Open Monday-Friday, Saturday by appointment. 409-336-7097.

Cleveland-Partlow House. 2131 Grand, Liberty. Now open to visitors on Tuesday from 10 a.m.-2 p.m. or by appointment. 409-336-5488.

WHERE TO EAT

Frank's Restaurant. 603 East US-90 (south side of US-90 east in Dayton). Nothing on the outside of this roadside restaurant would indicate that people drive from Houston and Beaumont just to eat seafood, chicken, or steak here. $$. Open Wednesday-Sunday. 409-258-2598.

La Colina Mexican Restaurant & Club. 2315 Highway 90, Liberty. Situated on historic Mexican Hill where Mexican prisoners were kept after the battle of San Jacinto, this restaurant follows suit by naming many of its specialties after specific prisoners. Quality Tex-Mex, with good gringo food tossed in to cool things off. The Mexican pizza crosses ethnic lines. Open daily. $-$$; □. 409-336-3677.

Brick's. This is a local favorite for barbecue, either by the plate, pound, or in sandwiches. Small deli and salad bar also. Two locations: FM-563 (open daily, 6 a.m.-7 p.m.) and 1804 Sam Houston, one block from the courthouse in Liberty, (open Monday-Friday). $-$$. 409-336-9190; 409-336-3166.

WANDERING THE BACKROADS

After viewing the local sights, continue this day trip to the Big Thicket via Moss Hill, Batson, and Saratoga. From Liberty, take T-146 15 miles north to Moss Hill, turn east (right on T-105) to Batson, and then northeast (left) on FM-770 to Saratoga.

Moss Hill is a farming and ranch area, named for the Spanish moss draped in the surrounding woods. Batson was a small village called Otto prior to the discovery of the Batson Oil Field in 1903 and was the scene of the Batson Round-up. The Round-up refers to gathering together all the unmarried women and auctioning them off to prospective husbands. It's a bit of a racy story, so ask locally or check out the pictures from the event at Heritage Garden Village in Woodville (Trip 2, this sector).

Saratoga was named for the famous New York State spa because it had several medicinal hot springs. A hotel catering to the health seekers burned decades ago, but some of the old foundation still can be found. Saratoga today is the gateway to the Big Thicket.

BIG THICKET

The Big Thicket National Preserve is the biological crossroads of North America, a unique place where the flora and fauna mix from all points of the compass. Ferns, orchids, giant palmettos, mushrooms, virgin pine — the abundance and variety is unequaled anywhere.

Unfortunately, many folks visit what they think is the Big Thicket and come home wondering what all the shouting is about. The problem is that there are twelve Big Thickets in the preserve, composed of eight land sections and four river/stream corridors and spread out over 84,550 acres and seven counties. The beautiful, biologically unique portions lie well beyond the highways.

Those statistics refer to acreage either within or earmarked for the National Preserve. In general terms, the Big Thicket area covers 3.5 million acres of southeast Texas.

All Texans love a tall tale, and the Big Thicket has its share. One concerns the Kaiser Burn-out at Honey Island near Kountze. Local residents called Jayhawkers who had no sympathy for the Confederate side of the Civil War hid out in the woods to escape conscription. Charged with capturing them, Confederate Captain James Kaiser set a fire and flushed them out. Two were killed, a few captured, and the rest vanished once again. Some claim the descendants of those Jayhawkers still live in the depths of the Big Thicket. As more people explore this wilderness there may be an update on the story.

And then there's the mysterious light that spooks travelers on the Bragg Road, a pencil-straight graded lane which follows the old railroad right-of-way between Saratoga and Bragg. Sometimes called a ghost or the Saratoga light, it appears as a pulsating phenomena and has been seen by enough people to warrant serious consideration. Some say it is the ghost lantern of a railway worker killed on the old line, and other less imaginative types claim it's just swamp gas. Whatever, it adds to the Big Thicket mystique.

In addition to the backroads route to Saratoga listed in the previous Day Trip, Houstonians have several ways of getting to the area. The most direct route follows US-90 east to a left turn on FM-770 north at Raywood, continuing on to Saratoga. An alternate is to take I-10 east to Hankamer, then north on T-61 to US-90. Turn west 4 miles to FM-770 north to Raywood. Depending on what unit of the Big Thicket you want to visit, there also is access from Woodville, Kountze, Cleveland, and Beaumont. A good state map is indispensable.

WHERE TO GO

The Turkey Creek, Beech Creek, Hickory Creek Savannah, and Big Sandy units of the national preserve are open to visitors. The Nature Conservancy operates the Roy E. Larsen Sandylands Sanctuary near Kountze. Big Thicket Association operates Rosier Memorial Park in Saratoga.

Turkey Creek is noted for changing habitats and carnivorous plants. There is a visitor information center on FM-420, 2.5 miles east of US-69 between Warren and Kountze. The Kirby Nature Trail is here, a 1.7- or 2.4-mile loop walk down to Village Creek and back. The information center is open daily, March-December; Thursday-Monday during January and February. It often closes early on Friday. 409-246-2337.

For a longer hike, the 9.2-mile Turkey Creek trail begins on FM-1943, about 3 miles east of US-69, and ends on County Line Road, slightly east of the intersection of FM-3063 and US-69.

Beech Creek, off FM-2992 southeast of Woodville, is a 4,856-acre beech-magnolia-loblolly pine plant community. However, a 1975 beetle epidemic killed almost all of the loblolly pines, so the forest is not as pretty as it was. A 1.5-mile loop trail passes through a mature stand of hardwoods.

The Hickory Creek Savannah unit, one-half mile west of US-69 and FM-2827 on a dirt road, combines the longleaf pine forest and wetlands with the dry, sandy soil found in the uplands. The Sundew Trail (1 mile) is open to the public, with a one-half mile trail under construction for the handicapped.

The Big Sandy Creek unit includes a rich diversity of plant and animal life. The 5.4 mile Woodland Trail, northwestern edge of the unit (near the Alabama-Coushatta Indian reservation), covers a flood plain, dense mature mixed forest, and upland pine stands. The trail entrance is not well marked, 3.3 miles south of US-190 on FM-1276. The trail also offers two shorter loops.

The Roy E. Larsen Sandylands Sanctuary is on T-327, 3 miles east of Kountze. Although it is considered an excellent example of the arid sandylands, it has 9 miles of frontage along Village Creek. A 6-mile trail is open daily, and guides can be arranged by writing to P.O. Box 909, Silsbee 77656, or calling 409-385-4135.

The Rosier Memorial Park Trail is a one-half mile loop through a palmetto-hardwoods plant community on the western outskirts of Saratoga near the intersection of FM-770 and FM 787. Open daily, and guides can be arranged through the Big Thicket Museum (see below).

WHERE TO START

The Big Thicket Museum on FM-770 in the tiny town of Saratoga has exhibits, slide shows, maps, and free advice. Open Tuesday-Sunday; Monday, by appointment. Information: Box 198, Saratoga 77585; 409-274-5000.

All-day canoe trips (fee) and in-depth hikes are offered on weekends and are listed in free brochures available by request from the museum. There are also five interpreter-guides, each specializing in some particular phase of the Big Thicket area. If you prefer to visit the Big Thicket on your own, stop at the museum for a map and orientation and then head for one of the six units listed previously. Do remember that this is a young park, expanding slowly on limited funds and that many of the areas are recovering still from man's earlier abuse.

A membership in the Big Thicket Association is available (same address as the museum). Members receive the Big Thicket Bulletin and schedules of special events, plus the satisfaction of aiding the growth and conservation of this unique preserve.

THINGS TO DO IN THE BIG THICKET

Birding. Excellent, particularly from late March through early May when hundreds of species pass on their way north up the Mississippi flyway.

Photography. There is a great range of natural subjects, particularly with macro and long lenses. Most of the beautiful things are found in the deep shade, so bring high ASA film and a tripod. Several outstanding photographic books on the Big Thicket are available at Houston libraries and bookstores to start those creative juices flowing. Some of the Big Thicket Museum tours are designed for and led by photographers. Check with the museum for information. 409-274-5000.

Camping. Primitive backpacking for families and individuals only is allowed by free permit from the National Park Service (713-839-2689) in the Jackgore Baygall, Beech Creek, Big Sandy, and Lance Rosier units. Big Thicket Museum allows campers on its grounds by reservation only. 409-274-5000. Kitchen and shelter available to camping groups.

Fishing. Allowed in all waters. A license is required.

Hunting and Trapping. Allowed in specific areas. Permit required. For information and season details, write P.O. Box 7408, Beaumont 77706, or call 409-839-2689.

Boating. Small watercraft can be launched at several places on the Trinity River, Neches River, Pine Island Bayou, and Village and Turkey creeks. The water level fluctuates; check before you make firm plans. The national preserve organizes free trips several times a month with a naturalist guide. However, you must bring your own canoe, life jacket, paddles, etc. The preserve does provide shuttle service at the end of the trip back to the starting point. For information and reservations, call 409-839-2689.

The Big Thicket museum also sponsors Saturday and Sunday guided all-day canoe trips in the spring, summer, and fall. These usually focus on the more remote areas, and many do not finish until sunset. All gear is provided — just bring a big lunch. Another museum specialty is close-up canoe trips with specialists along for ornithology, botany, herpetology, etc. For information and reservations, call 409-274-5892 between 6 and 9 p.m. or write P.O. Box 198, Saratoga 77585.

Exploring the Big Thicket waterways on your own can be difficult. There are few take-outs, and much of the land bordering on the creeks is privately owned, making canoe folks subject to trespass charges. Livery rental agencies operate out of Kountze, 409-246-4481; Steinhagen (Dam B), 409-283-3257; Beaumont, 409-892-3600 or 409-833-5347; Houston, 713-522-2848; and Groves, 409-962-1241.

Hiking. Wear sturdy, water-repellent boots. Remember this is rain country at certain times of the year, and the shady trails often have standing water. Mosquito repellent is an absolute necessity. Remember to register your hike at every trailhead. Pets and vehicles are not permitted on any of the trails, and do not wander on your own. The Big Thicket has earned its name and it's easy to get lost.

WHERE TO EAT

In addition to the Homestead Restaurant in Hillister (Day Trip Two, northeast sector) you may be able to catch some good home cooking at the Big Thicket Museum. They cater to groups of 15 or more by reservation only, and may fit individual families or travelers into an already scheduled group. Call for costs and reservations. 409-274-5000.

EAST

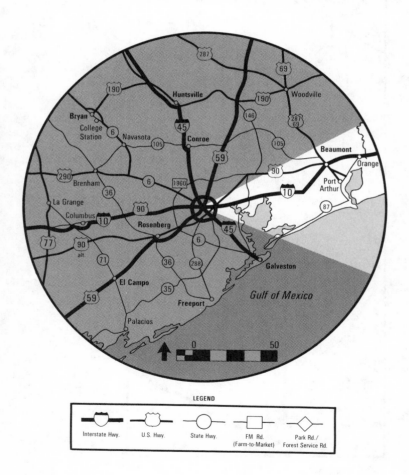

LEGEND

Interstate Hwy.   U.S. Hwy.   State Hwy.   FM Rd. (Farm-to-Market)   Park Rd./ Forest Service Rd.

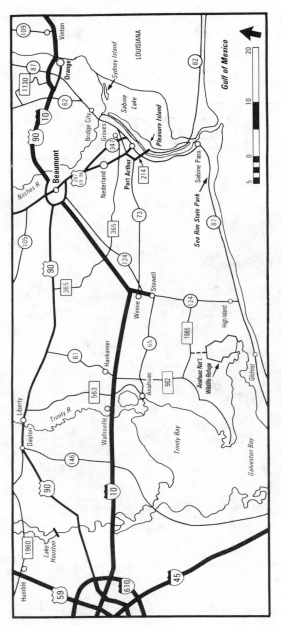

East: Day Trips 1, 2, and 3

Day Trip 1

BEAUMONT

BEAUMONT

The prospect of a day trip to Beaumont may evoke all the wild enthusiasm usually reserved for kissing your sister. But a little exploration in and around this river city can change your mind. There are a surprising number of things to do, not only in Beaumont proper but in the Golden Triangle Area (Beaumont/Orange/Port Arthur) that surrounds it. From Houston, there's only one way to get there — due east on I-10.

Although history hasn't painted the town with the color found in Austin's cradle country west of Houston, Beaumont is equally as old. The first land grant by Mexico to an Anglo in Texas was issued to Noah Tevis and covered 2,214 acres of richly forested area along the Neches River. Today, that is downtown Beaumont. By 1825 there was an active trading post here, and Jefferson County, of which Beaumont is the county seat, is one of the original counties formed by the Texas Republic in 1836. Since that time Beaumont has made its own brand of history in several ways.

Most vivid and important to modern America was the Lucas gusher at the Spindletop oil field in January, 1901, the greatest oil well in history. Almost overnight, Beaumont grew from 8,500 souls to 30,000 folks with advanced cases of oil fever, and a wooden shanty town called Gladys City was hammered into instant life on Spindletop Hill. By the end of that decade the oil was gone, and Gladys City was a ghost town of wooden shacks. Those glory days live again in the recreation of Gladys City, one-half mile north of its actual site and Beaumont's successful Bicentennial project.

Economically linked with the volatile oil and petrochemical industry, Beaumont has had its ups and downs. By the late 1960s, shifting financial fortunes had created another ghost town of sorts in the downtown area. But that scene slowly is changing, thanks to major commitments from both public and private sectors. During the past decade more than $120 million worth of capital improvements were made downtown, including new municipal and county government complexes. Work remains underway on multi-million dollar hotel and

117

office projects and a $5 million Art Museum of Southeast Texas. Other commercial projects involve the restoration of classic buildings listed on the National Register of Historic Buildings.

For free maps, brochures and advice, stop as you are entering Beaumont at the Visitor Information Center, I-10 at the Walden Road exit. Open Monday-Saturday; open Sunday also March-September. 409-842-1596.

A pre-recorded calendar of events called "What's Happening in Beaumont" can be dialed at 409-838-3634.

WHERE TO GO

Gladys City. At the intersection of University Drive and US-287. Although it lacks the grime of the original, this reconstruction is a good look at 1910 America as well as life in an oil boomtown. A rickety boardwalk connects most of the structures, just as it did in the oil fields.

The furnished replicas include a surveying and engineering office, the pharmacy and doctor's office, a photographic studio, a general store, and more. Vintage oil field equipment is scattered around, and the Lucas Gusher Monument is out back on its own site.

From I-10 take the US-287 turn-off to Port Arthur and then the Highland Avenue-Sulphur Drive exit. Signs take you from there. Fee. Closed Monday. For information write Lamar University Museum Services, P.O. Box 10082, Beaumont 77710. 409-838-8122 or 409-835-0823.

Spindletop Museum. Florida and Callahan streets on Lamar University campus. See exhibits about Beaumont before and after Spindletop, including geological and drilling information, and then combine this with a visit to nearby Gladys City. Free. Open Monday-Friday. 409-838-8896.

Old Town. East of the intersection of Calder and Eleventh streets in Beaumont. When the first Gladys City was in its heydey, this portion of Beaumont was a highly desirable tree-lined residential neighborhood. Today, it still is. Some of the homes are magnificent, and many now house galleries, restaurants, and antique and specialty shops.

A free map and guide helps you find out what's what in this 30-block area. Pick one up at the Tourist Information Center or order it in advance from the Convention and Visitor's Bureau, Box 3150. Beaumont 77704. 409-838-1424. Another source of help is Old Town Tours, 2121 McFaddin, Beaumont 77701. 409-832-8242.

The French Trading Post. 2995 French Rd. This substantial museum was John J. French's trading post and home back in 1845, now restored and operated by the Beaumont Heritage Society. The beautiful setting is in the woods north of town. Take the Delaware exit from US-69/96/287 north, turn west, and watch for the signs. Take a right turn on French Road, and you're there. Fee. Open Tuesday-Sunday. 409-898-0348.

Port of Beaumont. 1255 Main St. You'll have a bird's view of the busy port from an observation deck on top of the Harbor Island Transit

Warehouse. Ask the security guard at the Main Street entrance for directions. This modern port handles more than 30 million tons of cargo annually. However, the far banks of the Neches River remain richly forested and undeveloped, just as they were when clipper ships stopped here a century ago. 409-835-5367.

Babe Didrikson Zaharias Memorial. Gulf Street exit off I-10. In her time this outstanding woman athlete put Beaumont on the map and the town repaid her with a love and admiration that live on since her death from cancer in 1956. This memorial museum chronicles a life and career that saw her six times named Woman Athlete of the Year by Associated Press. Free. Open daily. 409-833-4622.

Beaumont Art Museum. 1111 Ninth St. (Corner of Ninth and Ashley streets. Take the 11th Street exit off I-10 east.) This is a good collection of paintings, sculpture, and mixed media in a Southern Regency mansion. Free. Closed Monday. 409-832-3432.

The Belle of Beaumont. This 300-passenger launch cruises the Neches River from a mooring in Riverfront Park behind the civic center. Ninety-minute sightseeing cruises leave at 11:30 a.m. and 1:30 p.m., Monday-Saturday. Sunday offers a general sightseeing cruise at 1:30 p.m.; a brunch cruise at 11:30 a.m.; family day on the Belle at 3:30 p.m.; and a family dinner cruise at 6 p.m. Reservations are suggested. Call to confirm departure times: 409-832-6635.

WHERE TO EAT

The Gazebo. 6445 Calder. A good place for a soup/sandwich lunch Tuesday-Saturday, seafood or steak dinners Thursday-Saturday. $-$$; □. 409-860-3594.

The Green Beanery. 2121 McFaddin, at Sixth Street in Old Town. This restaurant offers tasty, unusual twists on classic dishes, and all the veggies are fresh and crisp. Several interesting shops share this old-home complex. Dinner reservations are required. $$; □. Open Monday-Saturday. 409-833-5913.

Carlo's. 2570 Calder. If you want to dine Italian and the spouse wants Greek, this is the place. They specialize in both. $$; □. Open Monday-Saturday. 409-833-0108.

Patrizi's Other Place. 2050 I-10 South between Washington and College streets. Instant fame via a *Texas Highways* magazine feature story hasn't dimmed this family restaurant. All dishes are based on the owner's recipes, from the more than 30 entrees to the homemade soup and freshly baked bread. Not bad for the folks who introduced Beaumonters to Coney Island hot dogs and pizza a generation ago! $$; □. Open daily. 409-842-5151.

The Palace. 10255 Eastex Freeway, north of town on US-69/96/287. If you fancy a steak broiled over mesquite, come here. Unless two of you can eat half a longhorn, order the cowgirl steak and an extra fork. Also here: a disco and theatre featuring some of the best country music acts in town. $$; □. Open daily. 409-898-7513.

Day Trip 2

ORANGE

(See map, p. 116)

ORANGE

Anyone who thinks chili is the definitive Texas dish hasn't been in
Orange for the International Gumbo Cook-off on the first Saturday in
every May. More than 20,000 folks mob this annual event, proving the
Cajun heritage thrives in this part of the state.

Other folks pass by Orange on their way to bet on the ponies at Delta
Downs Racetrack, just over the bridge in Vinton, Louisiana. Whatever
your reasons for day-tripping this way, stop to enjoy this neat little city.
Some 32 miles east of Beaumont and the last gasp of Texas on I-10
before you find yourself in "Luziana," Orange has some interesting
places to visit.

Officially founded in 1836, the city's traceable history really starts
about 1600 when the Attacapas Indians settled here. French fur traders
came a century later, followed by the Spanish, and the city's name
comes from this latter period. Early French and Spanish boatmen
looked for the wild oranges that grew along the banks of the Sabine
River. As with the rest of Texas, the Anglo settlers ventured across the
Sabine in the early 1800s, but little is left to mark those times. Most of
Orange's tourist attractions date from the prosperous lumber and
ranching days from 1880 to 1920.

Local information including a list of eight antique stores can be had
from the Orange Chamber of Commerce, Box 218, Orange 77630.
409-883-3536.

WHERE TO GO

W. H. Stark House. Green Avenue at Sixth Street at Stark Civic
Complex. Built in 1894, this massive Victorian home is a visual delight,
inside and out. A ten-year restoration project, this 15-room structure
can be toured only by advance reservation. No children are allowed.
Tours start in the carriage house where an excellent glass collection is

on display. Fee. For information, write P. O. Drawer 909, Orange 77630, or call 409-883-0871.

Stark Museum of Art. 700 Green Ave., across from the Stark House. William H. Stark was a prominent financial and industrial leader in Orange who married Miriam Lutcher in 1881. She began collecting European art in the 1890s, and her son Lutcher and daughter-in-law Nedda continued the family tradition with further emphasis on art of the American West and the Taos School of New Mexico. This contemporary museum was completed by the Starks in 1976 and houses the varied and impressive collection. Free. Closed Monday. 409-883-6661.

First Presbyterian Church. 902 Green Ave. One wonders what there would be to see and do in Orange without the Starks. This impressive domed building is another Lutcher/Stark contribution to the city and the first public building to be air-conditioned in the world. The power plant with an air-conditioning unit was installed during the church's construction in 1908. The handmade stained-glass windows are impressive, as is the entire interior of the church. Tours available for six or more by advance reservation. If you can't fit into those tour requirements, stop in for Sunday services. 409-883-2097.

Heritage House. 905 Division St. While not as elegant as the Stark House, this turn-of-the-century home is worth a stop. Not only is it furnished as an upper-middle-class home would have been in those times, there are several "see-and-touch" exhibits for children and historical items of interest. Fee. Closed Saturday and Monday. Information: P. O. Box 5, Orange 77630. 409-886-5385.

Farmer's Mercantile. Corner of Sixth and Division streets, just where it's been since 1928. Saddles rest next to bins of nuts and bolts, onion sets are offered just below packets of bluebonnet seeds, and horse collars line the high walls. Whatever you might need, it's here — somewhere. People have been known to dawdle here for hours, remarking on the old wood stoves and bottle cappers. You can't miss the place — just look for hay bales on the side on the sidewalk. Open Monday-Saturday. 409-883-2941.

Linden of Pinehurst. US-90 (Business route), just off I-10 west of Orange. When Mrs. Gladys Brown saw a famous Natchez ante-bellum home called Linden, she ordered its duplicate built in 1956 at Pinehurst, the Browns' ranch in Orange. With its furnishings and 48 acres of parklike grounds it was donated in 1976 to Lamar University by the Brown estate and is open to the public unless a special conference is being held on the premises. Note: the gate sign says "Pinehurst Ranch," and a nearby gate says "Lindenwood" which leads to a subdivision. Tours may be arranged through Brown Center of Lamar University, 4205 Park Ave., Orange 77630. 409-883-5599.

Eddie Brown's Christmas Tree Farm. One mile north of I-10 on FM-1130 (exit 869) between Orange and Vidor. Tired of having more needles than presents under your tree? These live and lush Virginia pines are reputed to hold their freshness at least a month after being cut. Many folks choose their tree between October 25 and November 15. They leave a deposit, then return to cut it prior to the holidays. The farm is open daily from October 24 to December 20. 409-745-1826.

For a list of other Christmas tree farms in the Orange area, contact the Orange County Agricultural Office, P. O. Box 1456, Orange 77630. 409-883-7740, ext. 308.

Delta Downs. Twenty miles east via I-10, then north on L-109. Slightly beyond the two-hour/110-mile limit, this track is still a good reason to visit the Beaumont/Orange/Port Arthur area. September through March is a thoroughbred only period; and April through Labor Day is strictly quarter horses. Non-stop buses from Houston leave Saturday and Sunday. The round-trip fare includes general admission and reserved grandstand seating. For bus information, call 713-222-1161. For Delta Downs information, write P. O. Box 188, Vinton, LA 70668, or call 800-551-7142 (toll-free from Texas).

Sabine Delta Farms. Nine miles north of Orange on old T-87. If you are interested in how crawfish and catfish are raised and harvested, call for directions. Although most of the crop is sold to wholesalers, owner Ray McClain retails a minimum of 10 pounds to visiting customers. He also farms Virginia pines on 65 acres, and Christmas tree selection begins the first weekend in November. 100 Pea Farm Road, Orange 77630. 409-746-3050.

WHERE TO EAT

Cody's. 3130 North 16th St., at I-10. Stop here for charcoal-broiled hamburgers, steaks, fresh quiche, and salads. $$; ☐. Open daily. 409-883-2267.

Ramada Inn. 2600 I-10 west. If you are eastbound, exit at 16th Street; westbound, exit at Adams Bayou. Folks come from as far as Beaumont for the Friday night seafood buffet, mountains of fresh shrimp or crawfish, depending on the season. $$; ☐. Open daily. 409-886-0570.

Crawfish Capitol. T-12 and T-62, Mauriceville. Live or cooked, this is the place to get crawfish. Bill Harris purges the little devils and then sells them live or serves them up in tasty Cajun style etouffe, gumbo, etc. Barbecued crab is another treat. Save time for a tour of the vats of crawfish outside. Open daily. $-$$. 409-745-3022.

Day Trip 3

NEDERLAND
PORT ARTHUR

(See map, p. 116)

NEDERLAND

When you want to fish or hunt in southeast Texas, you well could be headed to Port Arthur. From Houston, the most direct route is I-10 east to Beaumont, followed by a swing southeast on US-69/96/287. For the day-tripper there are several activity options in the area, but first, let's take a look at one of the smaller towns you'll pass on the way — Nederland.

You'll think you are in Cajun country when you drive up the main street of this small community — the local market is advertising fresh boudain (sausage). Then you see some Dutch names on stores and a windmill at the end of the street. Established as a railroad town in 1897, Nederland first was settled by Dutch immigrants who were soon followed by French settlers from the Acadiana area of southwestern Louisiana, and both ethnic groups make Nederland what it is today.

WHERE TO GO

Windmill Museum and La Maison des Acadian Museum. 1528 Boston Ave., in Tex Ritter Park. These adjacent museums keep the dual heritage of Nederland alive. The authentic Dutch windmill's first floor is devoted to mementos of a local boy who made the big time in country and western music — Tex Ritter — and the remaining two floors have a sparse but interesting collection of assorted cultural treasures. Best is the old pirogue, hollowed out of a cypress log prior to 1845 and in use until bought and donated to the museum in 1969.

La Maison des Acadian Museum honors the French Cajun culture. A Bicentennial project by local volunteers, this authentic replica of a French Acadian cottage has furniture to match. Both museums are open daily, March-Labor Day, and Thursday-Sunday thereafter through February. Information: Nederland Chamber of Commerce, 1515 Boston Ave., Nederland 77627. 409-722-0279.

WHERE TO EAT

The Schooner. US-69/96/287 at FM-365. Famous for stuffed flounder and stuffed red snapper steak, this restaurant also has a few stuffed fish and game trophies for decor. $$; □. Open daily for lunch and dinner. 409-722-2323.

PORT ARTHUR

Now continue southeast on US-69/96/287 for a look at Port Arthur itself. The Sabine and Neches rivers form a large lake which then empties into the Gulf of Mexico 8 miles south of Port Arthur, and the town sits on the northwest edge of Sabine Lake.

Settled as Aurora about 1840, it became Port Arthur in 1897 as the terminus of the Kansas City-Pittsburgh and Gulf Railroad, and the ensuing oil strike in nearby Beaumont ushered in Port Arthur's golden age of growth. Today, although this city is a large industrial and refining center, it has little of its rich past to show day visitors.

WHERE TO GO

Pleasure Island. In Sabine Lake. Follow signs to Gulfgate Bridge and Pleasure Island south of town and then across the Sabine-Neches ship channel. This multi-million dollar development is stirring things up here with more to come. For now, there are miles of free levees for fishing and crabbing, a marina and golf course, boat ramps, a hotel, spots for picnicking and camping, and a 10-acre concert park that hosts musicals and festivals late spring through fall.

Pompeiian Villa. 1953 Lakeshore Dr. Believe it or not, this is a billion-dollar house. Built in 1900 by Isaac Ellwood, the "barbed wire king," it later was sold to the president of Diamond Match Co. He in turn traded it for $10,000 worth of Texaco stock worth $1 billion on today's market — or so the story goes in Port Arthur. This pink stucco villa is listed in the National Register of Historic Places and owned by the Port Arthur Historical Society. Open Monday-Friday. Fee. 409-983-5977.

Sea Rim State Park. Twenty-three miles south of metropolitan Port Arthur on T-87. To see vast flocks of birds on the wing in sunrise light is unforgettable. Even seasoned hunters have been known to put down their guns in awe, although you'll rarely find one who will admit it. Thanks to enlightened management, the sea rim marshlands between Port Arthur and Galveston are treated as the natural resources they are. Important to the seafood industry as nursery grounds for shrimp and fish, they also provide a unique experience for the visitor.

Sea Rim State Park is far more than the usual seaside camping and sunning spot. With more than 15,000 acres, this is the third-largest state park in Texas. It is divided into two areas. The beach unit has camping with and without hook-ups; a main headquarters with restrooms; hot showers; concessions; an outstanding interpretive center and program; and a 3,640-foot-long boardwalk through the wetlands behind the dunes. Slide shows about Sea Rim's unique ecology are presented on summer evenings, but visits and questions are welcome any time of year.

The second unit is a pristine marsh, explorable only by small power boat or canoe. You may surprise a flock of herons or egrets, or see an alligator or two — unless they see you first. There are six camping platforms and observation blinds within the marsh. If you want to explore these wetlands, you can either take your own craft or rent near the park. You must file a float plan with the rangers and also have marsh maps to guide you. Information: P.O. Box 1066, Sabine Pass 77655. 409-971-2559 or 409-971-2963.

Fishing. From Port Arthur you can either fish in the lake or the fresh water bayous that feed it, or move out into the Gulf of Mexico through Sabine Pass. Top game fish are speckled trout, red snapper, mackerel, billfish, and tarpon. A license is required. For information on party boats, marinas, guides et al., contact the Port Arthur Convention and Visitors Bureau, 3401 Cultural Center Dr., Port Arthur 77642. 409-985-7822.

Hunting. This is prime territory for duck and geese hunting, with four areas open to the public at various times during the November-January season. For overall information, contact Sea Rim State Park, P.O. Box 1066, Sabine Pass 77655. 409-971-2559. Other areas open for public hunting include the Texas Point and McFaddin Beach national wildlife refuges (409-971-2909) and the J. D. Murphree Wildlife Management Area (409-736-2559).

For the best in private hunting, local folks recommend LaBove's, a 10,000-acre reserve now under the management of a third generation hunter. If you are new to the sport, this is an excellent place to learn. Information: P.O. Box 1104, Sabine Pass 77655. 409-971-2258.

Taylor Bayou. The primitive mysteries of a natural swamp can be explored by pontoon boat between April and October. Closed Monday. Call for information and directions. 409-794-1749.

Sidney Island. At the north end of Sabine Lake between the junctions of the Sabine and Neches rivers, this wild place is protected and accessible only by authorized boat. Created from spoil left from the dredging of the Sabine-Neches waterway in 1915, this small island has evolved into a protected natural habitat for thousands of birds, including the rare roseate spoonbill. Owned by the State of Texas and leased to the Audubon Society, mile-long Sidney Island is best seen through binoculars from Rob Bailey's Fish Camp. From T-87 in Bridge City, turn south on Lake Street and go to the end of the road, an interesting drive in itself through a sea rim marsh. October visitors get a bonus. Migrating Monarch butterflies come in on the Texas "Blue

Norther" storms and rest here overnight en route to Mexico. Sue Bailey is the game warden for Sidney Island and welcomes questions, although actual visits to the island by visitors are rare. Information: Box 11, Bridge City 77611. 409-735-4298.

WHERE TO EAT

Al's Seafood. 2120 Main in Groves. Not fancy, just a local favorite for shrimp and delicious red snapper. $$; □. Open Tuesday-Saturday. 409-962-4531.

Farm Royal. 2701 Memorial Highway (US-69/96/287). Putting this restaurant in a guidebook could be a great mistake. It may become so popular we won't be able to get in. It serves some of the best Cajun food in all the Golden Triangle area. Best bet is probably the crawfish dinner. $$. Open Monday-Saturday. 409-982-6483.

The Wharf Gallery and Restaurant. One mile east of Rollover Pass at Gilchrist. This former service station now is an arty and tasty haven serving dinners of seafood, squab, rabbit, and frogs legs. The owner may play concert piano while you dine, or you may be entertained by an operatic tenor, comedian, folk performer, or magician. Marine and American Indian art lines the walls. No liquor is served but you're welcome to bring your own. $$$; □. Reservations required. Open Wednesday-Sunday for dinner. 409-286-5850. (Note: Dining here can also be combined with a trip to the Anahuac Wildlife Refuge or to Galveston.)

Sartin's. T-87 in Sabine Pass. If you've never had barbecued crab, come here and bring a bib. Known throughout southeast Texas, Sartin's is real "down home," right to the rolls of paper towels on the tables. The seafood is almost unbeatable and almost immeasurable. $-$$. Open daily. 409-971-2158; 409-971-9242.

WANDERING THE BACKROADS

The most logical and swift access from Houston to the entire Golden Triangle area is via I-10 east. But if time is no problem and you prefer quiet country roads, detour south from the interstate just past the Trinity River bridge and explore Wallisville and Anahuac.

One of the oldest towns in Chambers County, Wallisville was destroyed in 1966 by the U.S. Army Corps of Engineers in preparation for a large dam that has not materialized. In 1979, the non-profit Wallisville Heritage Park Foundation was created to restore the old town and preserve the adjacent El Orcoquisac Archeological District. So far, only the old post office and school are back in business, but the townsite is lovely and the project is gaining momentum. A new museum building is open Monday-Saturday. 409-389-2457.

From Wallisville, take the Old Wallisville Road to its intersection with FM-563 and continue south to Anahuac. The road itself is a delight— no center stripe or traffic — and it's easy to imagine how things were in the old days.

Anahuac has some bits of history and a wildlife refuge, the latter of great interest to bird lovers. Some 30 species of ducks and geese winter here along with many shore birds and marsh mammals. On Monday, Wednesday, and Saturday during April, a special marsh buggy takes birders on quests for the rarely seen yellow and black rail. Free, but reservations required. In all, the Anahuac refuge has 20 miles all season road (12 additional miles in the dry season) and hosts 250 species of birds, 30-50 species of mammals, and an extensive number of reptiles. Maps and guides are available at the visitor contact station. For information and a birding list, contact P.O. Box 278, Anahuac 77514. 409-267-3337.

Settled in 1821, Anahuac still has traces of Fort Anahuac, built about 1831 by the Mexican government. This small, somewhat run-down park is at the end of Main Street on Trinity Bay. Two old homes of interest are on the courthouse square. The first is Chambersea, built in 1845 and notable for the Texas star window in its western gable. The second is an early doctor's office, floated in from its original site in Cedar Bayou and now used as a museum. For access to either place, ask at the county clerk's office.

To continue to the Golden Triangle area from Anahuac, either take T-61 north to I-10 east, or FM-562 south and FM-1985 east to T-124 south. This connects with T-87 at High Island. Turn left and continue along the coast to Sea Rim State Park, Sabine Pass, and Port Arthur.

That latter route also can lead to Houston via Galveston. At the High Island intersection with T-87, turn right to Bolivar and take the ferry (long wait on good weather weekends) to Galveston.

SOUTHEAST

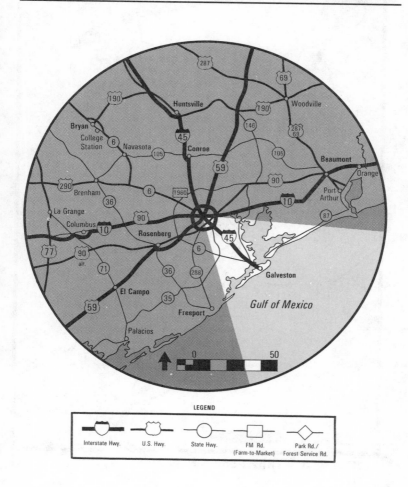

LEGEND

Interstate Hwy. U.S. Hwy. State Hwy. FM Rd. (Farm-to-Market) Park Rd./ Forest Service Rd.

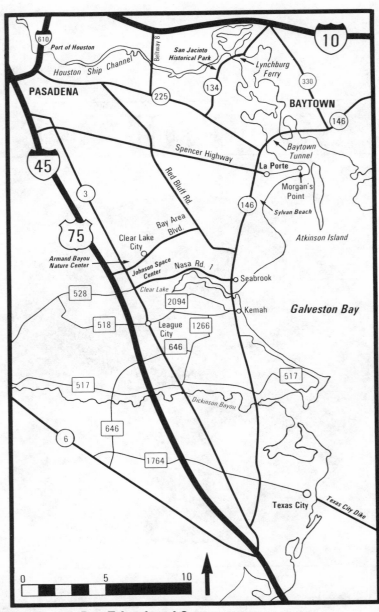

Southeast: Day Trips 1 and 2

Day Trip 1

PASADENA
BAYTOWN
MORGAN'S POINT/LA PORTE

PASADENA

As you drive southeast from Houston on I-45 and look east to the vast industrial-chemical complex that is Pasadena today, it's hard to believe that this once was projected to be Houston's garden. This bucolic feature was altered permanently by two events: the completion of the Houston Ship Channel as a deep-water port in 1915, and the discovery of oil in nearby Baytown in 1916.

Slightly off the usual Sunday drive itinerary, this upper bay region has several things to see and do. Start with a tour of the Port of Houston and the ship channel, and then head east on T-225 to digest some history at San Jacinto Battleground State Historical Park in La Porte. From there, ride the free Lynchburg ferry to Baytown and return to the Morgan's Point/La Porte area via the Baytown Tunnel. Here you'll find crabbing, swimming, bird-watching — all at a laid-back pace.

WHERE TO GO

Port of Houston. 7300 Clinton Dr. (Clinton exit from Loop 610 east). There's a free observation deck on the northwest side of the turning basin that is open daily, but a boat tour is better. The free 90-minute trip aboard the *M-V Sam Houston* takes you close to huge ships from around the world, grain elevators, refineries, docks — the active heart of the third-largest port in America. This is an official inspection vessel, and reservations are required. Make them at least three months in advance by writing to P.O. Box 2562, Houston 77252. Closed on Monday and for two weeks in April and the month of September. 713-225-4044.

The Beltway 8 Bridge. Accessible either from I-10 on the north or T-225 on the south. No reservations are needed here, just some toll change for a fantastic birds-eye view of the port from atop the bridge.

Gilley's. 4500 Spencer Highway, Pasadena. The Astrodome put Houston on the tourist maps, and Gilley's did the same for Pasadena as the locale for the movie *Urban Cowboy*. Now suburban cowboys in three-piece suits do the Cotton-eyed Joe and Two-step right along with the local rednecks. If it matters who is performing on stage, give them a call before you go. The amount of the cover depends on who is featured. Open daily. 713-941-7990.

LA PORTE

Founded by French settlers in 1889, this modest community's boundaries now stretch north to include the state's most significant historical site. See this portion of La Porte now, en route to the Lynchburg Ferry, and the Sylvan Beach sector on the final leg of this trip.

San Jacinto Battleground State Historical Park. From Pasadena continue east on T-225 to T-134. Turn north to Park Road 1836. Here, in just 18 minutes, Sam Houston and his ragged Texas Army defeated the Mexican Army in 1836. Not only did this change the future of Texas but that of the western half of continental America. The dramatic story is chiseled in granite and unfolds as you walk around the base of the 570-foot-tall San Jacinto Monument. There is no better capsule lesson in Texas history. Inside, an excellent museum has artifacts from the Spanish-Mexican period (1519-1835) and the Anglo-American settlement years (1835-1881). The museum is free, but there's a charge to ride the elevator to the top of the monument. Open daily. 713-479-2431.

A free map will guide you to markers and various positions of the Texas and Mexican armies on the battleground flanking the monument. This oak-tree-studded park land also has numerous picnic sites along one neck of the bay and the ship channel, so bring your lunch and your crabbing gear.

Battleship Texas. Near the battleground cemetery. Moored here since 1948, this is claimed to be the only surviving heavily armed dreadnought class battleship — a relic of both world wars. Fee. Open daily. 713-479-2431.

Lynchburg Ferry. From the cemetery and picnic area of the battleground park, continue northeast on T-134 to this free ferry, a relic from pre-freeway times. You are welcome to park your car and take the 15-minute round-trip ride as a passenger, or you can line up your car to be boarded along with others for each run. Open 24 hours a day, year-round. 713-424-3521.

Sylvan Beach. On T-146 in the bay-front portion of La Porte. This somewhat ramshackle county park has a playground, picnic areas, lighted 1000-foot fishing pier, and free boat launch. There also is good crabbing and safe swimming for children, but the entire park needs maintenance. The old train depot at the park's entrance is being restored to serve as a heritage museum sometime in the future. 713-471-1123.

WHERE TO EAT

San Jacinto Inn. T-134 across from the Battleship *Texas*, La Porte. Although there are several other good restaurants in the area, dining here is a well-established tradition. Most folks don't get past the platters of fresh boiled shrimp, crab, or raw oysters (depending on the season), which is a pity. The best of the lot may be the fried chicken and hot biscuits that follow the fish platters in this all-you-can-eat place. No menu, just mounds of food served family-style. The dress is informal, but no bathing suits or cut-offs, please. Reservations may cut your waiting time. $$$; □. Open daily except Monday for dinner, lunch also on Sunday. 713-479-2828.

Monument Inn Restaurant. 2710 Battleground Rd., La Porte. This is another favorite noted for its shrimp, steaks, and fish dinners. The huge aquarium is fascinating to adults as well as children. $$; □. Open for lunch and dinner daily. 713-479-1521.

BAYTOWN

From the San Jacinto Monument area, the Lynchburg Ferry takes you across the ship channel to Baytown where you continue on T-134 to Decker Drive (T-330). Turn southeast (right) and drive through Baytown. At the intersection with R-146, turn west (right) and return to La Porte via the Baytown Tunnel.

Both the Lynchburg area and Baytown were early Anglo settlements, the former an important trading post and the latter originally a sawmill and a store. Baytown boomed after the Civil War and now is a thriving industrial-residential community.

WHERE TO GO

Baytown Historical Museum. 3530 Market. An interesting look at the area's past. Free, but donations are welcome. Open Tuesday-Friday and on Sunday, 1-5 p.m. 713-427-8768.

MORGAN'S POINT

Back in those good old days, Morgan's Point combined with La Porte to provide a beach and bay playground for Houston. Big name bands brought crowds to the dance pavilion at Sylvan Beach, and folks drove around Morgan's Point just to see the handsome homes on the "Gold Coast."

A drive along Bayridge Road still takes you by some of those places, among them a grand replica of the White House, built by Texas Governor Ross Sterling. It has been a landmark on the Houston Ship Channel for generations. At the end of Morgan's Point is an undeveloped beach area, well known to birders. With binoculars, you can watch roseate spoonbills and other species on Atkinson Island in this upper portion of Galveston Bay.

WANDERING THE BACKROADS

You can easily delete tours of Baytown, La Porte, and Morgan's Point, and substitute either a jaunt to Wallisville/High Island/Bolivar (see Backroads section, Trip 3, east sector) or Activities of Trip 2, this sector.

Day Trip 2

CLEAR LAKE
SEABROOK/KEMAH
TEXAS CITY

(See map, p. 128)

CLEAR LAKE

A drive south from Houston on I-45 brings you to NASA Road One. Turn east to explore Clear Lake and the laid-back towns of Seabrook and Kemah.

The launching of sputnik also launched America's space program and created the Lyndon B. Johnson Space Center, part of the National Aeronautics and Space Administration. This is one of the biggest visitor attractions in the Clear Lake area, and the second largest tourist attraction in Texas.

After following man's exploration of space, you can challenge some new frontiers on your own. A few miles away is nature at her most primitive, a wilderness bayou seemingly untouched by man. Nearby, a local air field offers lessons in sky diving, and you can arrange a ride in the jump plane to test it out. The less adventurous can sail on Clear Lake or stop at the docks in Seabrook and Kemah for fresh shrimp.

WHERE TO GO

NASA-Lyndon B. Johnson Space Center. From I-45 south, take NASA Road One exit and go 3 miles east. This focal point for America's manned space flight program is both interesting and exhausting. A full tour requires about three hours of standing and walking, so come well fed and in comfortable shoes.

Most visitors start at Rocket Park, impossible to miss alongside the parking lot. From here, you walk to the Visitor Center and begin a self-guided tour that includes the main museum, two astronaut training areas, and the cafeteria/gift shop. Briefings are conducted in the Mission Control Center on a first-come/first-serve basis throughout the day. Check the tour schedule at the Information desk in Building Two upon arrival, and sign up for the next available briefing. You will want your camera and a flash unit to record the extensive displays of lunar material, space shuttle trainers, Apollo 17 spacecraft, the Mercury capsule, skylab trainers and other exotica. Free. Open daily (except Christmas Day). Information: NASA Johnson Space Center, Public Services Branch, AP4, Houston 77058. 713-483-4321.

Armand Bayou Nature Center. 8600 Bay Area Blvd. One of the last natural bayous around, this haven for wildlife is snuggled up to the Johnson Space Center on the south and Bay Area Park on the north.

Start first at the Nature Center and learn the territory through exhibits and a free slide show. Then walk some of the 5 miles of hiking trails around the center, either on your own or on a free guided hike twice a day on Saturday and Sunday. Also on the grounds is a three-acre working farm from the 1890s, complete with a restored and furnished farmhouse, barn and outbuildings, vegetable garden, and livestock. You can walk around the farm during the week or tour with a guide on Saturday and Sunday. There is no fee except for a special child's tour which must be reserved in advance. The nature center and grounds are open daily except for major holidays. No fee, but you may want to buy a family membership ($20) in the nature center. One of the benefits are rental canoes for members only. P. O. Box 58828, Houston 77258. 713-474-2551.

Exploring the bayou. You can float through this wilderness in a canoe or on the free pontoon boat trips operated by Harris County and departing from Bay Area Park, adjacent to the nature center. These free rides leave twice a day, Wednesday-Sunday, year-round, weather permitting. No children under three are allowed, and reservations are required. 713-326-6539.

In addition to the put-in at Bay Area Park, there's canoe access to the bayou from the NASA Road One bridge at Clear Lake Park. A free canoeing map is available from the nature center.

Excursions on the bay. The *Sundowner* trawler leaves from Capt. Wick's seafood restaurant, 318 11th St., Seabrook, on 90-minute bay cruises four times a day, Wednesday-Sunday. Fee. 713-474-5545.

Excursions on Clear Lake. The sailing catamaran *Obsession* offers sunset dinner cruises from a mooring behind Lakeside House, 3713 NASA Road One, Seabrook. 713-333-1355.

Sailing on Clear Lake. Half- and full-day rentals are available at Gulf Coast Sailing Center, 1206 FM-2094 on the south side of Clear Lake. If you've always had a hankering to sail but don't know how, these folks will give you a two- or six-hour in-water course and have you skimming along on your own in a day. 713-334-1722.

Windsurfing/Sailboarding. Lessons and rental equipment at Gulf Coast Sailing Center (previous entry) and Windsurfing Gale, 18105 Egret Bay Blvd. 713-333-9225.

Fishing and Pleasure Boating. For a complete list of all boat ramps, bait and fuel spots, marinas, and charter party boats, contact the Clear

Lake Area Convention and Visitor's Bureau, 1201 NASA Road One, Houston 77058. 713-488-7676.

Additional Canoeing. Dickinson Bayou roughly parallels FM-517 west to east from I-45. You'll find a good put-in and parking at the T-3 bridge in Dickinson, and then you have your choice of take-outs: either a carry at the FM-646 crossing (3.5 miles) or at Cemetery Road. This last section is the most beautiful and undisturbed.

Skydiving. At the Spaceland Paracenter at the Houston Gulf Airport on FM-1266 east of League City. Observers are welcome, and usually there are plenty of people around to explain what is going on. If you want to ride along in one of the jump planes, it's best to arrange it in advance (fee). The six-hour weekend classes include a skydive on your own. Take exit 20 from I-45 and turn east on FM-1266 for one-half mile. Open Thursday-Sunday. 713-337-1713.

SEABROOK AND KEMAH

From Clear Lake, take NASA Road One east and turn south (right) in Seabrook on T-146. Go over the bridge, turn left, and you are in Kemah.

This fishing village is a mecca for shrimp lovers and boat watchers — the channel under the bridge is the only passage from Clear Lake into Galveston Bay. If you want to buy shrimp fresh and relatively cheap off the boats, go early in the morning and shop around for the best price. The shrimp usually come "heads on," and you'll need an ice chest to cart them home. There's more good shrimp shopping on the Seabrook side of the bridge.

WHERE TO EAT

Louie's on the Lake. 3813 NASA Road One, Seabrook. Mix a huge all-you-can-eat seafood buffet with a handsome lakeside patio setting, and you have a winning combination. $$-$$$; □. Reservations advised. Open for dinner Tuesday-Sunday. 713-334-2502.

The Shrimp Hut. 1818 NASA Road One, Seabrook. It's crawfish in the spring, shrimp in the summer and fall, and oysters on the half-shell in the winter at this small family-run place. Watch for it on the north side of the road just before the railroad tracks and the intersection with T-146. There's some air-conditioned counter space inside, but most folks prefer the patio area in the back. You also can buy steamed crab and shrimp here, to eat or pack home. $. Open for lunch and dinner, Tues.-Sun. 713-474-5701.

Joe Lee's Down on the Creek. Second and Kipp streets, Kemah. Casual indoor and outdoor dining on good gulf seafood and steaks. The oyster bar is a local favorite. Open daily for lunch and dinner. $-$$; □. 713-334-3711.

South Texas Smokehouse. NASA Road One at Highway 146, Seabrook. Texas barbecue with all the trimmings is the specialty of this rustic place. Buffalo is Friday's specialty, followed by cabrito on Saturday. Open daily except Sunday for lunch and dinner. $. 713-474-4877.

Alfredo's Italian and Seafood Restaurant. 2360 NASA Road One, Seabrook (across from the Lakewood Yacht Club). Good food, including soft shell crab and gumbo, plus an oyster bar. Opera singers tune up at 7:30 p.m. on Friday-Sunday. Open daily for lunch and diner. $-$$; □. 713-474-7270.

Webb's Cove. 1913 NASA Road One, Seabrook. Owner-chef Lois Webb's inventive ways with local fish have landed her recipes in *Gourmet* magazine. House specialties include prime steaks and a shrimper skillet. $$; □. Open daily for lunch and dinner. 713-474-4740.

TEXAS CITY

Continuing south on T-146 from Kemah ultimately brings you to heavily industrial Texas City before connecting with I-45 just north of the causeway to Galveston Island. At that point you can continue on with Trip 3 in this sector, or swing north on the freeway toward home. But first, explore a bit around this port town.

Orginally an 1880s settlement called Shoal Point, Texas City is of interest to day-trippers primarily for its 5-mile dike jutting out into Galveston Bay. The winds are fairly dependable here, so the beach areas along the dike are filled with windsurfers, small sailboats, and catamarans whenever the weather says "sailing."

Fishing and crabbing are wherever you find a spot, and there also are boat-launching facilities, bait and tackle shanties, some cafes, and a lighted fishing pier. However, the dike often is unpleasant with debris, and there are few amenities such as restrooms, parking areas, or drinking water.

The dike is easy to find — just drive east through town on FM-1764 (Palmer Highway), turn right at the end of the road, then left onto the dike road.

WHERE TO EAT

Clifton By The Sea. From T-146 south, turn east (left) on FM-517 to the bay. The best reason for detouring to Bacliff is to eat fresh seafood and fine steaks at this former saloon, now spiffed up into a Nantucket-style family restaurant. Watch for the signs along T-146 between Kemah and Texas City. $$; □. Open Wednesday-Monday. 713-339-2933.

Gussie's Barbeque. Eleventh Avenue North and Nineth Street in Texas City. These folk serve everything from sandwiches and steaks to barbecue plate dinners with your choice of meats. $$; □. Open Tuesday-Saturday. 409-948-8004.

Day Trip 3

GALVESTON

(See map, p. 138)

GALVESTON

Cabeza de Vaca found it first. Later a pirate named Jean Lafitte made this sliver of island his base of shady operations in 1817. Legend says his treasure still lies buried in the shifting sands, and hunting for it with metal detectors is a favorite Galveston pastime.

To Houstonians, this small city, one hour's drive south via I-45, traditionally has been a relief valve, a chance to escape from big city life for a lazy day or weekend at the beach. But Galveston is far more than surf and sand. As the city's advertising says, "...the rest is history."

Long before Houston was much more than a landing on Buffalo Bayou, Galveston was a major port and the threshold to Texas for thousands of immigrants. By the 1870s it was the wealthy and thriving "Queen City of the Southwest," and during the golden era of 1875 to 1900 some of the most remarkable architecture in America lined its streets.

A devastating hurricane in 1900 killed some 6,000 people and swept much of the city out to sea. Vulnerable to every passing storm, Galveston seemed doomed to follow the earlier ports of Indianola and Lavaca into oblivion. To save the city and insure its future security, two massive engineering projects were undertaken, each remarkable for its time. The first was a massive seawall, 17 feet tall and 10 miles long, and the second was the raising of all the land behind that seawall from 4 feet to 17 feet.

These projects took seven years and were followed by yet another economic blow in 1915 when the successful completion of the Houston Ship Channel began to draw off the cream of the port trade. Galveston never recovered its pre-hurricane commercial importance, and ultimately it degenerated into one of the wildest gambling towns in the state. The Texas Rangers finally brought down the law in the 1950s, and after that, Galveston slumbered along as a rather seedy seaside city.

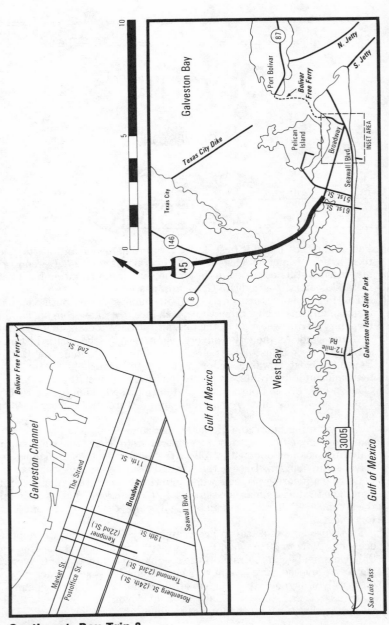

Southeast: Day Trip 3

But all is changing and on the upswing once again. The renovation and restoration of many historic buildings and Houston's burgeoning population have sparked fresh capital investment, and Galveston now is thriving.

WHERE TO GO

Exploring the Beaches. There are 32 miles of beachfront on the island and a variety of options. The decisions start after you cross the causeway from the mainland on I-45 and see the directional signs for East and West beaches. If you continue east (left lanes), I-45 becomes Broadway Boulevard and runs the length of the island. If you follow the signs for West Beach from I-45, you will cross the island on 61st Street to Seawall Boulevard, the island's second main drag. Turn right. West Beach starts where the seawall ends, and the road becomes FM-3005 at this point. Vehicular traffic on the beaches is restricted year-round.

One of the best things to happen to West Beach are three new beach park facilities on FM-3005. Here you'll find changing rooms, showers, food concessions, playgrounds and picnic areas, all backed by protected natural dunes, which often are in bloom with seasonal wildflowers. Horseback riding, parasailing, and windsurfing often are available nearby on weekends.

Heading back toward town, FM-3005 becomes Seawall Boulevard. Numerous small beaches are tucked between the jetties. Stop and watch the dolphins roll in the offshore swells and then walk out on the jetties and chat with the fishermen. You'll also find several places to rent roller skates, bicycles, or surreys, and the seawall itself is a grand promenade. This boulevard curves at the east end of the island and intersects Broadway at Stewart's Beach. This city-run stretch of sand is popular with families because it has lifeguards, a bath house and lockers, parking, concessions, etc.

A short drive farther east brings you to R.A. Apffel Park at the extreme end of East Beach. A recent $2-million bond issue funded a general clean-up here and new public facilities.

Galveston Island State Park. West of downtown Galveston on FM-3005 at the intersection with 13 Mile Road. Another beach facility with picnicking and camping, this 2000-acre state park also offers bird watching from observation platforms and nature trails along its north boundary which faces protected Galveston Bay.

Exploring Historic Galveston. Start at The Strand, once called the "Wall Street of the Southwest" and now considered the largest and best collection of 19th-century iron-front commercial buildings in America. To get there from Broadway, turn north on Rosenberg Avenue (25th Street — just look for a statue in the middle of the street) and drive for eight blocks. Most of the buildings along The Strand now house shops, galleries, businesses, and restaurants — the renaissance is in full swing. The Dickens-on-the-Strand Festival the first weekend in December is great fun, too. (See Special Events.)

Stop first at the Strand Visitor's Center, 2016 Strand, operated by the Galveston Historical Foundation in the restored Hendley Row (1856-60). Brochures outlining walking and biking tours are available here, along with audio-guide equipment (fee) and information on Galveston's points of interest.

Open daily. You also can get advance information by writing GHF, P.O. Drawer 539, Galveston 77553. Call 409-765-7834 or 713-488-5942. Some of the highlights include:

The Tremont House. 2300 Ship's Mechanic Row. A superb 1879 building now houses one of the most elegant small hotels in Texas. 409-763-0300; 713-480-8201; or 800-874-2300 (reservations).

The 1871 League Building. Strand at Tremont. One of the nicest restorations in the city and home to several interesting shops and The Wentletrap Restaurant (see Where to Eat listing).

Galveston Arts Center. 2127 Strand. If you like mixing art with history, drop in here. This is the old First National Bank building, restored to its 1866 grandeur, and the free gallery seems right at home. Open daily except Tuesday. 409-763-2403.

The 1877 Marx and Kempner Building. 2100 block of The Strand. Did you spot the clever trompe l'oeil mural? The original detailing of this building was removed decades ago, and what looks like an ornate and original facade actually is hand-painted artwork.

The 1882 H.M. Trueheart & Co. Building. 210 Kempner. This is one of the most ornate and distinctive structures in the area.

The Elissa. Pier 21, one block off The Strand. The oldest ship in Lloyd's Register of Shipping, this 1877 square-rigged barque still sails several times a year and is the third-oldest merchant ship afloat. The acquisition of the ship and its restoration are stories in themselves; be sure and see the *Elissa* film at the Strand Visitor's Center. Visitors can roam the restored after-cabins, the hold (self-guided tour), and the decks. Alongside, but on land, is a pint-sized playship for children and The Sail Loft museum shop. Open daily, unless she's at sea. Fee. Information: P.O. Drawer 539, Galveston 77553; 713-488-5942 (toll-free from Houston); 409-763-1877.

The area between piers 19 and 22 is home to Galveston's mosquito fleet, a colorful flotilla of shrimp trawlers. The annual Blessing of the Fleet and the Strand Festival each April turn the entire dock/Strand area into one vast party. Don't miss it, and bring your camera.

The Center for Transportation and Commerce. Strand at 25th Street. Here visitors can step into a replica of the old Galveston train depot and then move through a mini-series of light and sound shows depicting Galveston from the 16th century through the present day. Next comes the depot's original waiting room where there are life-size sculptures of travelers frozen in a moment of 1932. Out back are restored steam locomotives, assorted railroad cars, a snack bar and picnic gazebo, and some exhibits of steam-powered machines. Open daily, year-round. Fee. 409-765-5700.

Galveston County Historical Museum. 2219 Market St. More on Galveston's glorious past can be found here. Free. Open daily except Sunday. 409-766-2340.

The East End Historical District. Although almost any of Galveston's streets has its share of interesting buildings, this historical district covers 40 blocks of Victoriana in the general area bounded by Broadway, Market, 19th, and 11th streets. It can be driven or walked, but the best way to see the most is by bicycle or on the historical foundation's Homes Tour in early May. The best place to start a tour is:
   The Bishop's Palace. 1402 Broadway. Designed by noted Galveston architect Nicholas J. Clayton and considered one of the 100 most outstanding residential structures in America, this home was built between 1887 and 1892 for the Walter Gresham family. Even more interesting than its turreted, rococo exterior are the details and furnishings inside. Fee. Guided tours are given daily year-round (closed on Tuesday, September-June). 409-762-2475.

The Silk Stocking Historical District. This nine-block area is loosely bounded by Rosenberg, J and N avenues, and Tremont Street. Brochures available at the Strand Visitor's Center, the Galveston Island Convention and Visitor's Bureau, and Ashton Villa designate the best of the historic homes. One of the most striking is:
   Ashton Villa. 2328 Broadway. This Italianate beauty was built in 1859 of bricks made on the island and survived both a disastrous island-wide fire in 1885 and the 1900 storm. It now is restored as the showplace of the Galveston Historical Foundation. The tours begin in the carriage house with an excellent film on the city and the 1900 storm. Open daily, June-August; open Wednesday-Monday, September-May. Fee. 409-762-3933.
   1839 Samuel May Williams Home. 3601 Bernardo de Galvez (Ave. P). One of the two oldest structures in Galveston, this charming restoration now looks as it did in 1854. Tours include audio dramas that tell Williams' story as you move from room to room. Open daily. Fee. 409-765-1839.
   Antique Doll Museum. 1721 Broadway. Special display rooms in a restored cottage in the classical revival style. Open Tuesday-Sunday. Fee. 409-762-7289.
   J. F. Smith House. 2217 Broadway. This 1885 Italianate revival home now welcomes guests for bed and breakfast as well as tours. Open daily. Fee. 409-765-5121.

Galveston Today. If you've had it with history or are burned out with beaches, there is still plenty to do including:
   Treasure Isle Tour Train. Hop aboard at Moody Center, 2106 Seawall Blvd. (21st Street). You'll get a 90-minute, 17-mile guided tour of Galveston, both old and new. Fee. Open daily, weather permitting, May-August; Tuesday-Sunday, in March-April and September-

Tuesday-Sunday, in March-April and September-November. 409-765-9564.

Galveston Flyer. This replica of an old trolley leaves from 24th and Seawall on a one-hour tour of the city's highlights. Fee. 409-763-0884.

1894 Opera House. 2020 Post Office St. Restoration of this lovely old building is far enough along so that it can now host an eight-month art series and special events. 713-480-1894 or 409-765-1894.

Mary Moody Northern Amphitheatre. Galveston Island State Park, west on FM-3005 at the intersection with 13 Mile Road. Nightly performances featuring historical dramas and Broadway favorites are offered Memorial Day through Labor Day weekends. Tickets are available at Houston ticket centers and at the gate. A barbecue dinner is served before the performance. Fee. There is no play on Monday night. 409-737-3442.

Strand Street Theatre. 2317 Mechanic. This local repertory theatre has something on the boards almost every weekend, year-round, plus children's theatre as well. 409-763-4591.

Seawolf Park on Pelican Island. Accessible from Broadway via a north turn on 51st Street. Adults can enjoy watching Galveston's busy harbor from this unusual vantage point, and the children may scramble over a series of naval exhibits including an airplane, destroyer escort, and submarine. Also here: the *Selma,* one of the ill-fated ships built of cement as an experiment during World War I. It ran aground here years ago. Fee.

There is no swimming at Seawolf Park, but there are excellent facilities for fishing and picnics. Open daily, dawn-dusk. No fee, but there is a charge for parking.

Sea-Arama Marineworld. Seawall Boulevard at 91st Street. In addition to performances by trained dolphins and sea lions, you'll see one of the most appealing sea life aquariums in the country. A series of brightly lighted tanks hold rare aquatic species in a round exhibit room, the center of which is a 160,000-gallon salt water oceanarium. Sharks, turtles, stingrays, and other sea life swim by only inches from your face, and you can watch divers feed them by hand. There's also a comedy water-ski show (summer only) and a playground. Fee. Open daily, year-round. P.O. Box 3068, Galveston 77553. 409-744-4501; 713-488-4441 (toll free from Houston).

Fishing. In addition to the rock jetties along the seawall, there are commercial fishing piers at 25th, 61st, and 90th streets and at Seawolf Park on Pelican Island. Surf fishing is allowed along most of the open beaches. Your catch might be speckled trout, flounder, catfish, or redfish.

Many party boat operators offer trips into the bay or gulf, most leaving early in the morning from either the Galveston Yacht basin on the Strand between 2nd and 6th streets or the Pier 18-19 area, on the Bayfront between 18th and 19th streets. A Texas fishing license is required for everyone between the ages of 17 and 65 unless you are fishing at least 10.5 miles offshore. Check to see if a license is required before you board the boat. Common gulf catches include red snapper, sailfish, pompano, warsaw, marlin, ling, king mackerel, bonito, and dolphin. Take some seasick pills before you go — the gulf can get rough.

The Galveston Convention and Visitor's Bureau has lists of party boat operators. Here are two with Houston telephone numbers: Reel Fun Charters (deep sea fishing in the gulf), 713-771-4725; and Galveston Party Boats (bay and jetty fishing), 713-222-7025.

Carriage Rides. Authentic horse-drawn surreys leave from the Strand Visitors Center and the Hotel Galvez parking lot at 21st and Seawall on 30- and 60-minute tours of the Strand and historic districts. Fee. 409-763-7084.

Harbor Boat Tours. "The Colonel," a new but old fashioned stern-wheeler, churns its way around Galveston harbor on two hour cruises daily. Lunch is served aboard while it is berthed at pier 22, and a dinner/jazz cruise swings on Friday and Saturday evenings. Fee. 409-763-4900.

Two-hour narrated tours of the city's international port and water playgrounds are offered by Galveston Party Boat Tours twice daily in summer. Fee. 409-763-5423.

Sailing, Surfing, and Waterskiing. Try T-Marina at Washington Park, 61st Street at Offatts Bayou, for water-skiing lessons and tows or rental of windsurfers and/or small sailboats by the hour.

Special surfing areas are marked along Seawall Boulevard. Observe the warning signs, please.

Tennis and Golf. Information on specific locations for each is available from the Convention and Visitor's Bureau, 2106 Seawall Blvd., Galveston 77550. 409-763-4311.

WHERE TO EAT

Shrimp & Stuff. 39th and Avenue O. Beach-weary folks love this simple place for its tasty shrimp Po-Boys, homemade gumbo, and fish dinners. $-$$; □. Open Monday-Saturday. 409-763-2805.

Clary's. 8509 Teichman, across from the *Galveston Daily News*. Don't judge this place by its low-key exterior. Locals say it serves some of the best seafood on the island, often with a Creole touch. $$-$$$; □. Slightly dressy — no beach clothes, please. Open Monday-Saturday. 409-740-0771.

Gaido's. 3800 Seawall. Whether it's fried, broiled, or boiled, the fresh seafood here is excellent, partly because the dressings and sauces are made from scratch. $$-$$$; □. Open daily. 409-762-0115.

Hill's Pier 19. 20th and Wharf streets. Almost always crowded, this is the place for fresh fish, salads, gumbo, and more served cafeteria style. You can eat inside or up on the top deck overlooking the boat basin. $-$$; □. Open daily. 409-763-7087.

Wentletrap. 2301 Strand. Many Texans consider this the finest restaurant in the state. Housed in the historic and beautifully restored League Building, erected in 1871, the Wentletrap boasts an inventive menu and unusual decor. Come dressed for dinner. $$$; □. Open daily. 713-225-6033 (toll free from Houston); 409-765-5545.

Benno's. 1200 Seawall Blvd. Just what the beachfront needed — fast food service with quality behind the scenes. Owned by the former general manager of Gaido's, Benno Deltz, this sparkling blue and white place serves absolutely fresh blue and stone crab, crawfish fresh and etouffe, and other sorts of pisces. Very casual, so come in your swim suit if you wish. $-$$; □. Open for lunch and dinner daily. 409-762-4621.

The Captain's Table. 11126 San Luis Pass Road. A good place beyond the sea wall for standard seafood at affordable prices. Open daily for lunch and dinner. $-$$; □. 409-744-0881.

Donna's Downhome Diner. 2101 The Strand. Just what mom would fix, in the heart of the historic district. Open daily for lunch and dinner. $-$$; □. 409-763-4535.

Le Paysan. 2021 The Strand. Elegant food at moderate prices in a French cafe setting. This has been crowded since it opened, so you may want to come for the continental breakfast or high afternoon tea. Open Tuesday-Sunday. $$-$$$; □. 409-765-7792.

WANDERING THE BACKROADS

Driving southwest on FM-3005 the length of the island brings you to great fishing at San Luis Pass. Go over the causeway, and it's another 38 miles to Surfside Beach and Freeport. For activities there, see Trip 1 in the Southwest sector of this book.

Heading east from Galveston along the coast to Sea Rim State Park (East sector, Trip 3) is possible. Just take the free Bolivar ferry and continue on T-87. In Galveston, the Bolivar ferry slip is at the end of 2nd Street (turn north of Broadway), but don't try it on a prime-time weekend unless you love waiting in long lines.

Once on Bolivar, you won't find much, which is its biggest attraction — just some fishing camps, a long and primitive beach, and an abandoned lighthouse built in 1872. The lighthouse and its small homes were used as sets for the filming of *My Sweet Charlie*.

Watch for signs to the newly developed Fort Travis Seashore Park, on the right as you exit the ferry from Galveston. Long known as the place where Jane Long, the "Mother of Texas," gave birth to the first Anglo child on Texas soil, the fort was built before the turn of the century, raised and fortified after the 1900 storm, and pressed into military service during both world wars. Now renovated, it offers 1800 feet of new and protected beach for swimming, excellent fishing off the rocks, picnic and overnight camping areas, and small cabanas for overnight stays. On the second weekend of every month, volunteers share the fort's historical significance with all comers. Dressed in World War I and II military garb, they explain assorted war equipment, reenact American and German war strategies, and tour visitors through the cleaned out gun bunkers. 409-684-0333 (park) or 409-766-2411 (Galveston County Parks Department).

Directory

STATE PARKS, FORESTS, CAMPGROUNDS, AND TRAILS
CANOE ROUTES
HISTORIC SITES AND SPECIAL ATTRACTIONS
CELEBRATIONS AND FESTIVALS

STATE PARKS, FORESTS, CAMPGROUNDS, AND TRAILS

KEY:

AB	Airboat Rides	F	Fishing
BC	Bicycling	G	Golfing
BCH	Beaching	H	Hiking
B	Boating	HB	Horseback Riding
BR	Boat Ramp	N	Nature Trail
BW	Bird Watching	P	Picnicking
C	Canoeing	PG	Playground
CR	Crabbing	PN	Park Naturalist
E	Entertainment	S	Swimming
		WS	Water Skiing

Northwest

ALL AREA CODES 409 EXCEPT WHERE NOTED.

Apolonia Trail. Eight miles east of Anderson on FM-2819. Three loops provide scene changes through different habitats. Lengths: ¼ mile, 1.2 mile, and 1.9 mile

Huntsville State Park. Watch for park exit sign on I-45, 8 miles south of Huntsville. This piney park surrounds 210-acre Lake Raven. 191 campsites, some with full hook-ups. The 30 screened shelters must be reserved in advance. P.O. Box 508, Huntsville 77340. 295-5644. B, S, C, F, BC, N, BW, H, P.

Jones State Forest. West of I-45 on FM-1488. P.O. Box 2230, Conroe 77301. 756-6644. P, N, F, S.

Neches Bluff Overlook. From Loop 304 in Crockett, take T-21 northeast 23 miles, then Forest Service Road 511 southeast 2 miles

DIRECTORY   149

and a local road southeast one-half mile. One acre of camp area with flush toilets, grills, and some other facilities. Fee. Davy Crockett National Forest, Loop 304 East, Crockett 75835. 544-2046.

Ratcliff Lake. On T-7, 20 miles northeast of Crockett, 80 wheeled camper sites, plus another three-acre camp area. Flush toilets, grills, cold showers, canoe and paddleboat rentals, bait, picnic shelters, snack bar, laundry, and summer programs in an amphitheatre. No motor boats. Fee. Davy Crockett National Forest, Loop 304 East, Crockett 75835. 544-2046.

Lake Somerville State Park:

Birch Creek Unit. From T-36, go west 7.6 miles on FM-60, then 4.3 miles south on Park Road 57. 133 camper/tent sites with electricity and water hook-ups, flush toilets, showers, grills, pavilions. 535-7763. S, F, B, H, BW.

Nails Creek Unit. From US-290 in Burton, take FM-1697 northwest 7.6 miles. Turn east on local road for 2.4 miles, then southeast on local road for 1.2 miles (all are signed). 40 camper/tent sites with electric and water hook-ups. Flush toilets, showers, and grills.

Information on both from Lake Somerville State Park: Route 1, Box 61C, Ledbetter 78946. 289-2392. H, BR, S, F, WS, BW.

Lake Somerville. There is camping at the following four Corps of Engineers camps at various spots around the lake, most with hook-ups:

Big Creek. Four miles west of T-36 on FM-60, then 3.5 miles south on local road; watch for signs. There are two campgrounds here, one operated by a concessionaire and one by the Corps of Engineers. The first has 100 wheeled camper sites with water and electricity, 70 tent sites, six cabins, showers, and bathhouse. The Corps of Engineers section has 66 wheeled camper/tent sites with water, pit toilets, cold showers, and bathhouse. Route 1, Box 200-A, Somerville 77879. Fee. 596-6030 or 596-1622. B, H, S, F, BR, BC, P, WS.

Overlook. Two-tenths mile west on FM-1948 from T-36, then ½ mile northwest on local road; watch for signs. Concessionaire campground has 92 wheeled camper sites with electricity and water (some sewer hook-ups) plus 30 cabins. Another 30 sites are for tents, and general camping is allowed on another 25 acres. Pit toilets, showers, boat rental, bait, picnic shelters, tables, snack bar, ice, grocery, laundry, and bathhouse. P.O. Box 606, Somerville 77879. Fee. 289-2651. S, N, H, BC, B, BR, BW, F, WS, P.

Rocky Creek. Four miles west of T-36 on FM-1948, then 1.2 miles east on a park road; watch for signs. Some 155 wheeled camper or tent sites, some with water and electric hook-ups. Pit toilets, showers, picnic shelters. Fee. P.O. Box 548, Somerville 77879. 596-8811. BC, B, BR, BW, F, H, P, S, WS.

Welch. Follow signs on FM-1948 from T-36, then north on a local road 3.5 miles to the north end of the dam. 27 tent sites here, no hook-ups. Pit toilets, picnic shelters. Fee. P.O. Box 548, Somerville 77879. 596-8811.

Stubblefield Lake Recreation Area. From I-45 at New Waverly exit, take FM-1375 11 miles and turn northeast 2.9 miles on Forest Service Road 215. 28 camper/tent sites in the Sam Houston National Forest. Flush toilets, cold showers, grills. Fee. Box 939, New Waverly 77358. 344-6205. F, N.

West

Stephen F. Austin State Park. West on I-10 from Brookshire for 8 miles; watch for exit sign. This park combines history with a variety of outdoor activities. 40 sites with full hook-ups, 40 additional tent sites, and 20 screened shelters. The Brazos River is nearby. P.O. Box 125, San Felipe 77473. 885-3613. BC, G, H, F, N, S.

Southwest

ALL AREA CODES 409 EXCEPT WHERE NOTED.

Bryan Beach State Recreation Area. Two miles southwest of Freeport on FM-1495, then 3 miles south along the beach. Unimproved, with chemical toilets and no water. No supervision or information on-site. Free. BW, BCH, S.

Brazos Bend State Park. 20 miles southeast of Richmond on FM-762. Abundant wildlife, plus 15 miles of hike/bike nature trails. Some 4,897 acres fronting on 3.2 miles of the Brazos River. Showers, flush toilets, primitive and hook-up campsites, observation towers, three small fishing lakes. Route 1, Needville 77461. 553-3243. BC, BW, F, H, N, P.

Lake Texana State Park. Six miles east of Edna on T-111 then jog north to the lake on a local road. Lakeside, this park has 141 sites, all with water, and 86 with electricity, showers, flush toilets, grills. Box 666, Edna 77957. 512-782-6691. BCH, B, BR, BW, F, H, P, PG, S, WS.

Northeast

ALL AREA CODES 409 EXCEPT WHERE NOTED.

Big Creek Trail. From Shepherd, take T-156 northwest to Forest Service Road 217 and turn east (right). The longest of the three loop trails here is 4.5 miles. P.O. Box 1488, Lufkin 75901. 632-TREE.

Bull Creek Trail. On US-287, 8.5 miles west of Corrigan. A 1.5-mile loop along the banks of Bull Creek in northwestern Polk County, outside of Corrigan. Maintained by Champion International, Box 1488, Lufkin 75901. 632-TREE.

Dogwood Trail. Three miles east of Woodville, off US-190. Winding along the banks of Theuvenin Creek, this trail is 1.5 miles long.

Double Lake Recreation Area in Sam Houston National Forest. From T-105 in Coldspring, take FM-2025 south ½ mile, then a local road southeast 1.5 miles. 55 camper/tent sites on Double Lake, plus flush toilets, cold showers, grills, and a concessionaire for boat rentals, ice, groceries, etc. Fee. Box 1818, Cleveland 77327. 713-592-6462.

Lake Livingston State Park. From Livingston, take US-59 south 2.3 miles, and turn southwest (right) on FM-1988. Follow signs. On the lake with 147 camper sites. Electric and water hook-ups. 10 screened shelters. Flush toilets, showers, tables, bathhouse, and lake aquatic activities. Route 9, Box 1300, Livingston 77351. 365-2201. B, BR, F, H, N, P, S, WS.

Longleaf Pine Trail. A 2-mile trail, 3 miles east of Camden on FM-62.

Lone Star Hiking Trail. Near Montague Church on FM-1725, north of T-105 between Cleveland and Conroe. This is a 27-mile segment of a 140-mile forest trail. Map is available from the San Jacinto District, Sam Houston National Forest, 407 N. Belcher, Cleveland 77327. 713-592-6462.

Martin Dies Jr. State Park. 15 miles east of Woodville via US-190 and Park Road 48 on B. A. Steinhagen Lake (Dam B Lake). 705 acres with lakefront campsites, some with utilities, some primitive. Screened shelters, restrooms, and showers. P.O. Box 1108, Dogwood Station, Woodville 75979. 384-5231. BR, N, H, F.

Moscow Trail. Between Moscow and Leggett on the east side of US-59. Two loops (½ mile and 1.5 mile) run along the banks of Long King Creek. P.O. Box 1488, Lufkin 75901. 634-5512.

Steinhagen Lake (Dam B): There are three unimproved Corps of Engineers campgrounds here, all with pit toilets. For information, write Star Route 1, Box 249, Woodville 75979. 429-3491. Specific locations are:

Campers Cove. From US-190, turn south 2.6 miles on FM-92, then east one-half mile on a local road. 25 wheeled camper/tent sites, plus 81 acres for primitive camping. Free. P, S, BR, B, WS.

East End. From US-190, turn south 4.4 miles on FM-777, then .3 miles on a local road. 6 tent sites, 6 wheeled camper sites. Fee. P, S, BR, B, WS.

Magnolia Ridge. From Woodville, go 11.7 miles on US-190 east, then .9 miles north on a local road, then 1 mile east on a local road. 36 camper/tent sites, some with electric hook-ups. Primitive camping on 570 acres. Dump station. Fee. P, S, BR, WS, B.

Wolf Creek Park on Lake Livingston. Accessible from both Livingston and Huntsville via US-190. Turn south on T-156 at Point Blank, then east (left) 7 miles on FM-224. From Coldspring, take T-156 north to FM-224 and turn east (right). On the wooded banks of the lake, this park has 69 tent sites with water, tables, and grills, plus 30 trailer sites with hook-ups. Reservations strongly advised, although there are seven overflow camping areas. Flush toilets, hot showers, bathhouses, laundry. P.O. Box 309, Coldspring 77331. 653-4312. F, B, S, WS, BR, P.

East

ALL AREA CODES 409.

Anahuac. Chambers County operates nine camping areas in and around Anahuac. For information, write Chambers County Road Department, P.O. Box 447, Anahuac 77514 (no telephone). Among the sites are:

Fort Anahuac Park. From I-10 take FM-563 south 7 miles, T-61 west 1 mile, then south on Main Street 1 mile. 6 wheeled camper sites with water and electricity, plus general camping on 20 acres. Flush toilets. Fee. S, BCH, F, BR, PG.

James H. Robbins Memorial Park. From I-10, take T-61 south 4 miles, FM-562 south 22 miles, Smith Point Road south 1 mile, and Hawkins Camp Road northwest 1.6 miles. General camping on three acres fronting Galveston and East bays. Flush toilets, cold showers, scenic views, and observation tower. F, BR.

Bun's Beach on Lake Anahuac. From I-10, take FM-563 south to Bay Lane. This 10-acre camp has no hook-ups but does permit beach camping. Flush toilets, water. Free. S, P, B, F, BR.

Double Bayou Park. From I-10, take T-61 south 4 miles, FM-562 south 7 miles, and Eagle Ferry Road west .5 miles. This 20-acre camp area is on the east fork of Double Bayou. Flush toilets, swimming, fishing, playground. Fee. P, S, F, BCH, PG.

Sea Rim State Park. From Sabine Pass, take T-87 west 9.4 miles to park entrance sign. One of the finest state parks in the system and directly on the Gulf of Mexico. There are 20 camper sites with water and electricity on the beach, and six camping platforms in the sea rim marsh. Excellent naturalist program, numerous activities, and airboat rides into the wetlands. Major interpretive center for the Texas coastal region. Box 1066, Sabine Pass 77655. 971-2559. PN, BCH, BR, BW, C, CR, F, N, S.

Tyrrell Park. From I-10 in Beaumont, take exit 848 and continue .5 miles on Walden Road to entrance sign. This 500-acre woodland has 92 camper sites with full hook-ups, a touch-and-smell garden for the blind, and a botanical center. Box 3827, Beaumont 77704. 838-0652. G, HB, PG, H.

Southeast

ALL AREA CODES 409 EXCEPT WHERE NOTED.

Galveston Island State Park. Six miles southwest on FM-3005. This extremely popular park fronts on both the Gulf of Mexico and west Galveston Bay. There are 170 camper/tent sites with hook-ups and 10 screened shelters. Facilities include showers, flush toilets, and grills. Activity options include wildlife observation platforms in the marsh, and outdoor dramas and musicals in amphitheatre. Route 1, Box 156A, Galveston 77550. 737-1222. F, B, H, BCH, BR, BW, CR, N, E.

Ft. Travis Seashore Park. On the southern end of Bolivar Peninsula, off T-87, two miles from ferry landing. Cabanas, campground, and picnic area, plus outstanding fishing, swimming and wildlife observation. Reservations accepted for cabanas. P. O. Box B, Port Bolivar 77650. 684-0333.

For general information about the Sam Houston National Forest, write to San Jacinto District, P.O. Box 817, Cleveland 77327. 713-592-6462.

For information on the Davy Crockett National Forest, contact the Neches District, Loop 304 East, Crockett 75835. 544-2046.

For information on state parks, wildlife, or fisheries, contact the Texas Parks and Wildlife Department, 4200 Smith School Rd., Austin 78744. 800-792-1112 (toll-fee).

The Texas Forestry Association puts out a booklet on woodland hiking trails no camper should be without. Box 1488, Lufkin 75901. 632-TREE.

CANOE ROUTES

Northwest, Trip 3: Brazos River in Bryan/College Station section.

West, Trip 3: Colorado River in Columbus section.

Southwest, Trip 1: Colorado River in Wharton section.

Trip 2: Bastrop Bayou in Angleton Section.

Northeast, Trip 1: San Jacinto river in Humble section.

Trip 2: Trinity River in Livingston section.

Neches River in Woodville section.

Trip 3: Village and Turkey creeks in Big Thicket section.

East, Trip 3: Sea Rim State Park in Port Arthur section.

Southeast, Trip 2: Armand Bayou and Dickinson Bayou
in Clear Lake section.

HISTORIC SITES AND SPECIAL ATTRACTIONS

Northwest

ALL AREA CODES 409 EXCEPT WHERE NOTED.

ANDERSON

Grimes County Courthouse. Top of Main Street. Impressive building with hand-molded brick and native limestone trim. Open Monday-Friday.

Steinhagen Log Cabin. Left of intersection of M-1774 and T-90. Built in 1852 by slaves; walls are unspliced, hand-hewed timbers. Open by arrangement with Historic Anderson, Inc. 873-2662.

BRENHAM

Giddings-Stone Mansion. Near South Market and Stone. A 12-room Greek Revival home built in 1869. Private residence.

Ross-Carroll-Bennett House. 515 Main St. This private residence typifies the fancy fretwork of the Victorian era (1893).

Giddings-Wilkin House. 805 Crockett. Built in 1843, this is thought to be the oldest house still standing in Brenham. Sometimes open as a museum. Contact Washington County Chamber of Commerce. 314 South Austin, Brenham 77833. 836-3695.

CHAPPELL HILL

Browning Plantation House. One mile south of US-290 off FM-1371. This three-story wood home was built in 1856 and is listed in the National Register of Historic Places. Tours for groups of four or more. Fee. 836-9515.

Chappell Hill Historical Museum and Methodist Church. On Church Street, one long block east of Main. Housed in an old school, the museum is staffed only from 1-5 p.m. on Sunday. The adjacent church has stained-glass windows of note and is open for Sunday services. No fee, but a donation is appreciated.

Stagecoach Inn. Main at Chestnut Street. Listed in the National Register of Historic Places, this Greek Revival structure was built in 1850 and was a busy stage stop during the Civil War. Guided tours for groups of four or more. Fee. 836-9515.

Winkelmann. Four miles east of Brenham. Shops and eateries in a collection of vintage buildings. Open daily. 836-3440.

CROCKETT

Davy Crockett Spring. West Goliad at the railroad underpass, west of the town square. The spring still flows and serves a public drinking fountain at what is thought to be Crockett's campsite.

Downes-Aldrich Historical Home. 207 North 7th St. Listed in the National Register of Historic Places, this Victorian survivor now is a historical and cultural activities center for Crockett. Information: Crockett Chamber of Commerce, 700 East Houston, P.O. Box 307, Crockett 75835. 544-2359.

Monroe-Crook Museum. 709 East Houston Ave. Built in 1854, this home is open for public tour on Wednesday mornings and weekend afternoons, March-December. No fee, but a donation is appreciated. 544-5820.

HUNTSVILLE

Henry Opera House. 12th and Avenue K. Built as a Masonic Hall in 1880, this building housed Huntsville's first department store on the lower level and opera house on the second floor.

Old Post Office. Between 12th and 13th streets on Avenue K. An interesting turn-of-the-century building. Open Thursday.

Sam Houston Memorial Park and Museum. Between 17th and 19th streets on Sam Houston Avenue. A museum housing the memorabilia of this legendary Texas statesman. Open daily except major holidays. No fee. P.O. Box 2054, Huntsville 77341. 295-7824.

Gibbs Powell House. 11th and Avenue M. Tours by arrangement of this 1862 home. 295-9500, ext. 17, or 295-5767.

INDEPENDENCE

Independence Baptist Church. At the intersection of FM-50 and

FM-390. The present Stone building was finished in 1872 and still holds services every Sunday. 836-5117.

Old Baylor Park and Ruins of Old Baylor University. One-half mile west of the Independence Baptist Church on FM-390. This birth site of Baylor University is a nice place to picnic.

Texas Baptist Historic Center. Adjacent to the Independence Baptist Church. Houses pre-Civil War artifacts and old church and family records. Open Wednesday-Sunday. No fee. Route 5, Box 150, Brenham 77633. 836-5117.

MONTGOMERY

The following homes are in the heart of Montgomery and are within walking distance of each other: Old Methodist Parsonage (1860s); Magnolia (1854); Cathalorri (1854); Yesteryear (1850s); Social Circle (1908); J. B. Addison Home (1882); Fernland (1830/1867); and the Arnold-Simonton Cottage.

TOMBALL

Tomball Community Museum Center. North of Main Street at the end of Pine Street. Clustered here are bits of the past collected by the Spring Creek Historical Society. Open Thursday-Sunday, spring-fall. Days and hours vary. No fee. 713-255-2148 or 713-351-7222.

SPRING

Old Town Spring. East on Spring-Cypress Road from I-45. This shopping district is filled with specialty shops, antique stores, flea markets, and galleries, most housed in quaint old homes. Open Tuesday-Saturday, 713-353-2317.

Hanna Barbera Land. One-half mile north of exit 68 (Holzwarth Rd.) from I-45. Family fun in Smurfland. Fee. 713-526-0914.

WASHINGTON-ON-THE-BRAZOS

Washington-on-the-Brazos State Historical Park. A handful of buildings mark this site that was the birthplace of the Texas Republic. Independence Hall was the site of the signing of the Texas Declaration of Independence. The Star of the Republic Museum (within the park) offers a slide presentation and self-guided tour. No fee. Open daily, March-Labor Day; closed Monday and Tuesday, September-February. P.O. Box 317, Washington 77880. 878-2461.

West

ALL AREA CODES 409 EXCEPT WHERE NOTED.

BROOKSHIRE

The Waller County Historical Museum. Fifth and Cooper streets. Built in 1913, this museum houses period furnishings, historical artifacts, and documents. Free, but donations welcome. Open weekdays except Thursday. 713-934-2826.

COLUMBUS

The Colorado County Courthouse. Bounded by Spring, Milam, Walnut, and Travis streets. Built in 1890 and 1891, this courthouse has recently been fully restored. Free. Open Monday-Friday.

Confederate Memorial Hall Museum. Housed in the old water tower on the southwest corner of Courthouse Square. Built in 1883, it houses exhibits and artifacts from early Columbus and from the "Old Three Hundred," as Stephen F. Austin's first colony was known. Open by appointment. Donation. 732-2571 or 732-5269.

Koliba Home Museum. 1124 Front St. Owned by former State Representative and Mrs. Homer Koliba, this 18-room private home was built between 1837 and 1838 and houses antiques and other memorabilia about Texas. Open daily; hours vary. Fee. 732-2913.

Stafford Bank and Opera House. On Spring Street, across from Courthouse Square. Built by millionarie cattleman R. E. Stafford in 1886, this elegant building originally housed Stafford's bank and a 1,000-seat theatre upstairs. Open Monday-Friday, and during the Magnolia Homes Tour in May.

EAGLE LAKE

Attwater Prairie Chicken National Wildlife Refuge. Six miles northeast of Eagle Lake on the west side of FM-3013. Open daily. No fee. P.O. Box 518, Eagle Lake 77434. 234-3021.

FAYETTEVILLE

The Red & White. On the Square. Built between 1853 and 1855, this is considered the oldest building on the square and is a good place to buy beer, wine, antiques, and handicrafts. Open Friday-Monday. 378-2722.

LA GRANGE

Fayette County Heritage Museum and Library. 855 South Jefferson St. across from the Faison home. Historic documents are preserved here. Free. Closed Monday and Thursday. 968-6418.

Hermes Drug Store. Across from the courthouse at 148 North Washington. Established in 1856, this is the oldest drug store in continuous operation in Texas. Open Monday-Saturday. 968-3357.

Monument Hill State Historic Site. Two miles south of town off US-77. This memorial to a historic Tex-Mex battle is a good picnic site, with restored buildings soon to open. Open daily. Fee. P.O. Box C, LaGrange 78945. 968-5658.

N. W. Faison Home, Museum, and Garden Center. 822 South Jefferson St. This frontier home is interesting for its architecture, antique furnishings and artifacts from the Mexican War. Open weekends, or by appointment. 968-5140.

ROUND TOP

Bethlehem Lutheran Church. Up the hill from Moore's Fort and one block southwest. Dedicated in 1866, this sturdy stone church features a pipe organ built of cedar. Open daily; no fee.

Festival Hill. One-half mile north of town square on T-237. Outdoor classical concerts here year-round, as well as special master classes in music during the summer. P.O. Box 89, Round Top 78954. 249-3129.

Henkel Square. On the town square. A collection of 13 historically important buildings on eight acres of land. Docents in each building explain the structure, its furnishings, and how it fit into early Texas life. Open daily except major holidays. Fee. P.O. Box 82, Round Top 78954. 249-3308.

Moore's Fort. Across T-237 from the town square. A double log cabin marks the frontier home of John Henry Moore, built about 1828 on another site in La Grange. No fee. Open daily.

SIMONTON

Roundup Rodeo. From I-10 west, take FM-1489 exit in Brookshire south for 10 miles to Simonton. Turn right on FM-1093 to the arena. Held every Saturday night, year-round. Fee. P.O. Box 329; Simonton 77476. 713-346-1534.

WINEDALE

Winedale Historical Center. Four miles northeast of Round Top via FM-1457 and FM-2714. This 190-acre outdoor complex houses 19th-century farm buildings, homes, a smokehouse, pioneer kitchen, old barn, and other frontier structures. Open Saturday and Sunday. Fee. (The grounds and picnic area are open daily at no charge.) In August, Shakespeare is performed in the old barn. Admission to the performances is free, and a reception follows the play. Saturday evening performances are preceded by a stew dinner served by the staff. Fee. Spring and fall festivals also are held on the grounds. P.O. Box 11, Round Top 78954. 278-3530.

Southwest

ALL AREA CODES 409 EXCEPT WHERE NOTED.

ANGLETON

Brazoria County Museum. 100 Cedar at North Velasco, inside the courthouse. A collection of artifacts from Brazoria's early days. Open Thursday-Saturday. No fee. 713-331-6101, ext. 1208.

BRAZOSPORT

San Bernard Wildlife Refuge. Ten miles west of Freeport on FM-2918. Best access to this 24,455-acre prairie and marsh preserve is by boat along the Intracoastal Canal. Limited land access for birding, wildlife photography, and nature observation. No fee. Open daily. P.O. Drawer 1088, Angleton 77515. 849-6062.

Brazosport Center for the Arts and Sciences. On the Brazosport College campus off T-288. Exhibits here interpret this coastal region through shells, plants, animals, fossils, minerals, and Indian artifacts. No fee. Open Tuesday-Sunday. 400 College Dr., Brazosport 77566. 265-7831.

EAST AND WEST COLUMBIA

Replica of the First Capitol. 14th Street, behind the post office. A recreation of the small clapboard building that served as the first capitol of Texas. Furnishings are to the period. No fee. Open Monday-Friday mornings.

Ammon Underwood House. On the river side of Main Street, East Columbia. Built about 1835, this is the oldest existing home in the East Columbia community. Furnishings and some of the wallpaper are original. Open during the San Jacinto Festival and by appointment. Contact Mrs. Gladys Gupton, 509 Bernard St., West Columbia 77486. 345-4213.

The Varner-Hogg State Historic Park. One mile north of T-35 on FM-2852. A two-story brick home survives today on land that was one of the original land grants from Mexico, given to the former owner, Martin Varner, in 1824. In 1901 the house became the home of the first native-born governor of Texas, James Hogg. The home was donated to the state in 1958 and restored in 1981. Fee. Open Tuesday, Thursday, and Sunday. P.O. Box 696, West Columbia 77486. 345-4656.

RICHMOND

The Fort Bend County Courthouse. Fourth and Jackson streets. Built in 1908, this is the only building in Fort Bend County listed in the National Register of Historic Places. Notable features are the three-story rotunda, mosaic tile floors, and rich woodwork. No fee. Open Monday-Friday.

Fort Bend County Museum. Fifth and Houston streets. Displays include artifacts of Carrie Nation, Jane Long, and other early Texas figures. A special exhibit room has a changing show of assorted archive and reserve materials. Museum staff will guide historical tours of Richmond by advance notice. Open Tuesday-Sunday. No fee, but donations appreciated. P.O. Box 251, Richmond 77469. 713-342-6478.

John H. Moore House. Fifth and Liberty streets. Built in 1883, this gracious home now is a museum noted for its furnishings. Fee. Guided tours on Sunday.

Decker Park. North of the railroad tracks at Sixth and Preston streets. Three buildings are here: a railroad depot, a log cabin replica, and a home once owned by Carrie Nation's daughter. The Victorian brick structure across Preston Avenue was the county jail from 1896 to 1948 and now houses the Confederate Museum. Exhibits include muskets, rifles, guns, and other Civil War memorabilia. No fee. Open Sunday and by special appointment. Contact the Fort Bend County Museum (above) for information.

Imperial Sugar Co. 198 Kempner, Sugar Land. From US-90A, turn north on Kempner, and park where there is space. This modern plant is housed on the site of the S. M. Williams cane plantation, established in the 1840s. You can watch sugar being processed from the raw product to store-ready package. Only groups need reserve a tour in advance. No fee. Open Monday-Friday, P.O. Box 9, Sugar Land 77478. 713-491-9181.

Arroyo Seco Historical Park. Southeast from Richmond on FM-762. Due to open soon, this park is a project of the privately funded George Foundation and will be devoted to the heritage of Fort Bend County. Call for days and hours of operation. Route 1, Box 577, Richmond 77469. 713-343-0415.

Northeast

ALL AREA CODES 409 EXCEPT WHERE NOTED.

COLDSPRING

San Jacinto County Museum. In the old jail, part of the Old Town Heritage Center. Small but interesting. Open Monday-Friday. No fee.

CLEVELAND

Big Creek Scenic Area. Six miles west of Shepherd, off T-150. Open daily. P.O. Box 1818, Cleveland 77327. 713-592-6462.

BIG THICKET

Big Thicket Museum. On FM-770, in the center of Saratoga. Houses, exhibits, slide shows, maps, and advice on this biologically diverse area. No fee. Open Tuesday-Sunday, Monday by appointment. Box 198, Saratoga 77585. 274-5000.

Visitor Information Center for the Big Thicket. On FM-420, 2.5 miles east of US-69 between Warren and Kountze. Call for seasonal days and hours of operation. 246-2337.

HUMBLE

Mercer Arboretum. 22306 Aldine-Westfield Rd. Some 214 acres filled with rare and beautiful plants. This bird sanctuary has a fern garden, picnic and demonstration garden areas, and more to come. Open daily; no fee. 713-443-8731.

LIBERTY

Geraldine Humphreys Cultural Center. 1710 Sam Houston Street in Liberty. Local and pioneer history and special art exhibits are featured here. No fee. Open Monday-Friday, Saturday. 336-8901.

Sam Houston Regional Library and Research Center. Four miles north of Liberty via T-146 and a northwest turn (left) on FM-1011. Valuable historical records, documents, portraits, and other artifacts from the days when Liberty was a major steamboat port on the Trinity River. No fee. Open Monday-Friday. 336-7097.

Cleveland-Partlow House, 2131 Grand. This Liberty showplace is open on Tuesday from 10 a.m.-2 p.m. Fee. 336-5488.

LIVINGSTON

Alabama-Coushatta Indian Reservation. On US-190, 17 miles east of Livingston. This is a 4,600-acre camping-recreation-tourist complex where you will see virgin forests, swamps, an Indian village replica where tribal members demonstrate early housing, crafts, foods, and dances. An open-air historical pageant is held Monday through Saturday nights, June-August. Fee. For reservations, call 563-4777. Days and hours vary. Route 3, Box 640B. Livingston 77351. 563-4391.

Polk County Museum. 601 West Church St. in Murphy Memorial Library. Exhibits from the early days of Polk County, plus Indian artifacts are here. Donation appreciated. Open Monday-Friday, 327-8192.

Colquitt's Syrup Mill. From Livingston, continue north on US-59 9 miles and turn east on FM-942 for 15 miles. Turn right on a dirt road and bear right again at the first fork. One of the few old-fashioned sugar cane mills left in east Texas, this operation runs full-tilt seven days a week from the second week in November until Christmas. No fee. 563-2340.

WOODVILLE

Heritage Garden Village. One mile west on US-190. A rambling conglomeration of Americana including the world's only flying outhouse, old log cabins, and an old newspaper plant. Open daily. Fee. P.O. Box 666, Woodville 75979. 283-2272.

Allan Shivers Library and Museum. Two blocks north of the courthouse at 302 North Charlton. This restored Victorian showplace houses papers, furnishings, and assorted memorabilia collected by Texas Governor Allan Shivers. Fee. Open Monday-Saturday, Sunday guided tours by appointment. 283-3709.

Jones County Music Park. Near Colmesneil on T-255. Weekend concerts from April through October bring country and western headliners to these east Texas woods. P.O. Box 730, Doucette 75942. 837-5463.

Lake Tejas. In Colmesneil, 11 miles north of Woodville via US-69 and FM-256. A delightful version of the old swimming hole. Open summers only. 837-5201 or 837-2225.

East
ALL AREA CODES 409 EXCEPT WHERE NOTED.

BEAUMONT

Babe Didrikson Zaharias Memorial. Gulf Street exit off I-10. This memorial museum chronicles the life and career of this famous athlete. No fee. Open daily, 833-4622.

The French Trading Post. 2995 French Rd. Formerly the home and trading post of John Jay French in 1845, this museum has been restored in a beautiful woods setting north of town. Open Tuesday-Sunday. Fee. Beaumont Heritage Society, 2985 French Rd. Beaumont 77706. 898-0348.

Gladys City. At the intersection of University Drive and US-287. A reconstruction of Beaumont's famous oil boomtown of 1910. Furnished replicas include everything from a livery stable and mortuary to a pharmacy and barber shop. Fee. Open Tuesday-Sunday. P.O. Box 10082, Beaumont 77710. 838-8122.

Spindletop Museum. Florida and Callahan streets on the Lamar University campus. Exhibits of Beaumont before and after Spindletop, including geological and drilling information. No fee. Open Monday-Friday, 838-8896.

Old Town. East of the intersection of Calder and 11th streets in Beaumont. Homes, restaurants, antique stores, and specialty shops are found in this 30-block area. A free map and guide are available from the Convention and Visitor's Bureau, Box 3150, Beaumont 77704. 838-1424.

The Belle of Beaumont. Moored behind Civic Center in Riverfront Park. This 300-passenger launch cruises the Neches River daily. 832-6635.

NEDERLAND

Windmill Museum. 1528 Boston Ave. in Tex Ritter Park. An authentic Dutch windmill houses local treasures here. The first floor is devoted to Tex Ritter mementos. No fee. Open daily, Labor Day-February. 722-0279.

La Maison des Acadian Museum. Next to the Windmill. French Cajun culture is honored here in this authentic replica of a French Acadian cottage. Open daily, Labor Day-February. Nederland Chamber of Commerce, 1515 Boston Ave., Nederland 77627. 722-0279.

ORANGE

Heritage House. 905 Division St. This turn-of-the-century home is furnished to the period with several "see and touch" exhibits for children. Admission fee. Open Tuesday-Friday, and Sunday afternoon. P.O. Box 5, Orange 77630. 886-5385.

First Presbyterian Church, 902 Green Ave. An impressive domed building, this is the first public building to be air-conditioned in the world (1906). Tours are available for six or more by advance notice. Otherwise, stop in for Sunday service. 883-2097.

W.H. Stark House. Green Avenue at Sixth Street at Stark Civic Complex. Built in 1894, this massive Victorian showplace can be toured by advance reservation. No children, please. Fee. Open Tuesday-Saturday. P.O. Drawer 909, Orange 77630. 883-0871.

Stark Museum of Art. 700 Green Ave., across from the Stark house. This contemporary museum houses a varied and impressive collection of art. No fee. Open Wednesday-Saturday, and Sunday afternoon. 883-6661.

Delta Downs. 20 miles east via I-10, then north on L-109. September through March offers thoroughbred racing only, and April through July is quarter horse time. Non-stop buses from Houston leave Saturday and Sunday, and the round-trip fare includes admission and reserved seats for the races. For bus information, call 713-222-1161. For Delta Downs information, write P.O. Box 188, Vinton, LA. 70668, or call 800-551-7142 (toll-free from Texas).

PORT ARTHUR

Pompeiian Villa. 1953 Lakeshore Dr. This billion-dollar house was built in 1900 by Isaac Ellwood. He traded it for $10,000 worth of Texaco stock worth $1 billion on today's market — or so the story goes in Port Arthur. Listed on the National Register of Historic Places. Fee. Open Monday-Friday. 983-5977.

Sidney Island. At the north end of Sabine Lake at the junction of the Sabine and Neches rivers. This small island has evolved into a protected habitat for thousands of birds, including the roseate spoonbill. Accessible only by boat; permit required. Write Game Warden, Box 11, Bridge City 77611. 735-4298.

Southeast

ALL AREA CODES 713 EXCEPT WHERE NOTED.

CLEAR LAKE

NASA-Lyndon B. Johnson Space Center. Three miles east of I-45 on NASA Road One. The focal point of America's manned space flight program, this center has tours and exhibits such as the Mission Control Center, the Space Environment Simulation Lab, lunar material, and Apollo 17 spacecraft. No fee. Open daily. NASA Space Center, Public Services Branch, AP4, Houston 77058. 483-4321.

Armand Bayou Nature Center. 8600 Bay Area Blvd. One of the last natural wilderness bayous around, this haven for wildlife is bounded by Johnson Space Center on the south and Bay Area Park on the north. No fee. Open daily, except major holidays. 474-2551. P.O. Box 58828, Houston 77058. Free pontoon boat tours are by reservation only: 334-1221.

Excursions on Clear Lake. The *Clear Lake Queen,* a replica of a Mississippi riverboat, roams the lake on weekends. For information, call 334-1515. A sailing catamaran, *Obsession,* offers sunset dinner cruises April through September. 333-1355.

PASADENA

Port of Houston. Clinton exit from Loop 610 east. A free observation deck on the northwest side of the turning basin is open daily, but the free boat tour is better. Call for days and hours of operation and for boat tour reservations. 7300 Clinton Dr., P.O. Box 2562, Houston 77252. 225-4044

LA PORTE

San Jacinto Battleground State Historical Park. Park Road 1836, north of T-134. The story of Texas' 1836 victory over Mexico is chiseled in granite at the base of the 570-foot-tall San Jacinto Monument. A museum also is on the premises, and the Battleship *Texas* is nearby. No fee. Open daily, year-round. 479-2431.

ALL AREA CODES 409 EXCEPT WHERE NOTED.

GALVESTON

The Center for Transportation and Commerce. Strand at 25th Street. A replica of the old Galveston train depot brings old-time Galveston to life. Fee. Open daily, year-round, 765-5000.

The Elissa. This tall ship for Texas is moored at Pier 21, one block off the Strand. Fee. Open daily. P.O. Box 539, Galveston 77553. 763-0027; 713-488-5942 (toll-free from Houston).

Galveston County Historical Museum. 2219 Market St. More on Galveston's colorful past can be found here. No fee. Open daily, except Sunday. P.O. Box 1047, Galveston 77553. 766-2340.

Mary Moody Northern Amphitheatre. Galveston Island State Park, west on FM-3005 at intersection with 13 Mile Road. Nightly performances of either the Lone Star historical drama or popular Broadway musical favorites are offered Memorial Day through Labor Day at 8:30 p.m. Tickets are available at Houston ticket centers. A barbecue dinner is served before the performance. Fee. No plays on Monday. 737-3442.

1894 Opera House. 2020 Post Office St. This old restored building now houses performing arts events. Contact the Galveston Arts Council, 763-6459, for hours and information.

Seawolf Park on Pelican Island. From Broadway, turn north on 51st Street. An exhibit of naval ships is here, plus fishing and picnicking. Open daily, dawn-dusk. No fee to the park.

Sea-Arama Marineworld. Seawall Boulevard at 91st Street. This sea life aquarium boasts a 160,000-gallon oceanarium and special dolphin shows. Fee. Open daily, year-round. P.O. Box 3068, Galveston 77553. 744-4501 or 713-488-4441 (toll-free from Houston).

The Strand. Turn north on Rosenberg Avenue from Broadway. The Strand Visitor's Center, 2016 Strand, is operated by the Galveston Historical Foundation. You'll find information on walking and biking tours here. The Center is open Monday-Saturday. P.O. Box 539, Galveston 77553. 765-7834 or 713-488-5942.

The Galveston Island Convention and Visitor's Bureau. 2106 Seawall Blvd. 77550. This is another good source of information on Galveston's attractions. 763-4311.

GALVESTON'S EAST END HISTORICAL DISTRICT

Bounded by Broadway, Market, 19th, and 11th streets. This district covers 40 blocks of Victoriana. The showpiece is The Bishop's Palace, below.

The Bishop's Palace. 1402 Broadway. Built between 1887 and 1892, this Nicholas J. Clayton-designed home is considered one of the 100 most outstanding residential structures in America. Fee. Guided tours are June-August, Monday-Friday; Sunday. Open daily, September-June (closed on Tuesday). 762-2475.

GALVESTON'S SILK STOCKING HISTORICAL DISTRICT

Nine blocks bounded by Rosenberg, J and N avenues, and Tremont Street. Here you'll find the following:

Ashton Villa. 2328 Broadway. Built in 1859, this Italianate beauty was made of island brick and is the showplace of the Galveston Historical Foundation. Fee. Open daily. Closed Tuesday September-May. Box 1616, Galveston 77553. 762-3933.

1839 Samuel May Williams Home. One of the two oldest structures in Galveston. Restored to its 1854 charm and a living museum. Open daily. 765-1839.

Antique Doll Museum. 1721 Broadway. Outstanding collection in a restored cottage. Open Tuesday-Sunday. 762-7289.

CELEBRATIONS AND FESTIVALS

JANUARY

Festival Hill: Concerts followed by dinner lure you to Round Top once a month from August through April — most welcome during the quiet days of January and February. The gourmet dinner is followed by a vintage film, and you can stay overnight in historic Menke House. Advance arrangements necessary. One-half mile north of the town square on T-237. 409-249-3129.

FEBRUARY

Galveston Mardi Gras: This reincarnation of a long-gone tradition keeps the island swinging the weekend before Lent. 409-763-4311.

Texas Independence Day: Washington-on-the-Brazos re-lives its brief moment in the Lone Star limelight every year on the weekend closest to March 2. 409-878-2461.

The Clear Lake Gem and Mineral Show. This event is one of the best of its kind in the country. 713-488-7676.

MARCH

Nederland Heritage Festival: Complete with a tulip pageant, parade, tennis tourney, flea market, and mini-marathon. On Boston Avenue, between 14th and 17th streets in front of the city hall. 409-722-0279.

The Dogwood Festival and Western Weekend: Woodville celebrates the beauty of spring in the East Texas woods with this annual event the last weekend in March and the first weekend in April. Everything from a parade and historical pageant to a beard contest, rodeo, and trailride. 409-283-2632.

Historical Tour and Antique Show: Some of Brenham's surviving ante-bellum homes can be toured during this event. 409-836-3695.

APRIL

Country Livin' Festival: Formerly Bellville's Bluebonnet Festival, this annual event falls on an early April weekend when the wildflowers around town are at their prime. The main action is in the mini-park, half a block south of the town square, but the chamber of commerce mans welcome booths around town where you can pick up packets of bluebonnet seeds and maps of driving tours to see the year's best color. At the park, expect mock Civil War battles, authentic Indian dances, Cajun music and food, folk artists, and buggy rides. 409-865-3407.

The Texas Trek: Anderson comes to life each spring to celebrate its history with a home tour, parade, and plenty of Main Street fun. 409-873-2662.

Montgomery Trek: Many of Montgomery's old homes open their doors to the public on a mid-April weekend. 409-597-4155.

Round Top Antique Fair: Annually on the first weekend in April antique dealers show their best in Round Top's old Rifle Association Hall. 713-520-8057.

Texas Crafts Exhibition: Combine a trip to the antique fair in Round Top with a stop at Winedale, just down the road, where you'll find quality exhibitions of the state's best handcrafts, plus folklife demonstrations, picnic, etc. 409-278-3530.

San Jacinto Day Festival: East and West Columbia celebrate the early days of the Republic with guided bus tours of old homes and plantations, the replica of the first state capitol, and a shrimp boil. 409-345-3921.

Brazos de Dio Western Fiesta: Bryan's big fling of the year, with entertainment, rodeo, and arts and crafts. 409-779-2278.

Triathalon: Biking, running, and swimming competition open to all comers (advance registration, please) in Bryan-College Station. 409-693-6552.

Pilgrimage Homes Tour: Calvert opens the doors of its marvelous old homes. If you love Victoriana and antiques, don't miss it. 409-364-2559.

Bluebonnet Antique Show: Chappell Hill shows off its old things in this best of Texas seasons. 409-836-3695.

Sylvan Beach Festival: La Porte revives its heyday with a parade, chili cook-off, and entertainment. 713-471-1123.

Blessing of the Fleet(s): Take your pick; Galveston and Freeport both host this festival annually. Freeport: 409-265-2505. Galveston: 409-763-4311. Galveston usually swings with the Rainbow Festival on the Strand in conjunction with the colorful parade of boats that officially opens the shrimp season. 409-763-2403.

Neches River Festival: Beaumont celebrates for a week with historical pageants, shows, exhibitions, etc., all over town. 409-838-1424.

The Good Oil Days Festival: Humble's streets are filled with crafts and entertainment on a mid-April weekend. 713-446-2128.

MAY

Czech Fest: Rosenberg celebrates its ethnic heritage every spring at the Fort Bend County Fairgrounds. 713-342-5464.

Maifest: Brenham hosts the oldest spring festival in the state in the heart of the wildflower season. 409-836-3695.

Kaleidoscope: Beaumont spreads out the best in creative arts and crafts on the art museum grounds. 111 Ninth St. 409-838-6581.

Homes Tour: Galveston's annual peek behind historic doors. One of the best in the state. 713-448-5942 (toll-free from Houston); 409-765-7834.

Magnolia Homes Tour: Columbus rolls back time the third weekend in May with a melodrama, parade, historic homes tours, plus antiques and crafts shows. 409-732-5881.

Old Town Spring: Country Fair time on the first weekend in May. 713-353-2317.

Navasota Nostalgia Days: Family fun, plus tours of several historic private homes. 409-825-6600.

International Gumbo Cook-Off: Orange and its Cajun folks relegate chili to the back burner in favor of every sort of gumbo brewed in the South, always held on the first weekend in May. 409-883-3536.

JUNE

Pow Wow: Livingston and the Alabama-Coushatta Indian Reservation are your destinations for this ethnic celebration. 409-327-4929; 409-563-4391.

Big Thicket Day: The tiny town of Saratoga swings annually with a bluegrass and country music party, plus country cooking, crafts, etc. 409-274-5000.

Sandcastle Building Contest: Freeport invites the public to try their hand at this timeless childhood art at Surfside Beach. 409-265-2505.

Fiddler's Festival: Some old-time toe-tapping music in Crockett on the second Friday in June. 409-544-2359.

June Feast: Cat Spring celebrates on the first Sunday of the month.

Fireman's Picnic: Frelsburg draws folks into town with this celebration on the second weekend of the month. 409-732-3716.

JULY

Fourth of July Celebrations: Just pick your town — the following all have their own versions of the old-fashioned Independence Day: Chappell Hill (409-836-6382); Clear Lake (713-488-7676); Columbus (409-732-5881); Huntsville (409-295-8113); Lake Jackson (409-265-2505); Navasota (409-825-6600); Crockett (409-544-2359); Round Top (409-249-3308); and Sealy (409-885-3222).

Annual Rodeo: Call Crockett's chamber of commerce regarding activities: 409-544-2359.

Ashton Villa's Old Fashioned Family Outing, Armadillo Longneck Festival and **Jean Lafitte Days:** All three enliven Galveston around the Fourth of July. 409-763-4311.

Lunar Rendezvous: The Clear Lake area celebrates with art shows, festivals, tournaments, and a decorated boat parade. 713-488-7676.

River Raft Race: Wharton makes good use of the mighty Colorado River on the Fourth of July. 409-532-1862.

AUGUST

Arts & Crafts Festival: Port Arthur hosts this salute to summer. You can also combine it with a trip to Sea Rim State Park. 409-963-1107.

SEPTEMBER

Antique Show: Cat Spring gathers the best of treasures in a country setting.

This is **county fair** month, so plan a trip to La Grange (409-968-5756); Columbus (409-732-5881); Brenham (409-836-3695); Woodville (409-283-2632); Hempstead (409-826-6118); or Beaumont (409-838-6581).

Pasadena Stock Show and Rodeo: This week-long event is held at the rodeo grounds, 7600 Red Bluff. 713-487-7871.

Spindletop Boom Days: Beaumont's oil days live on at this annual shindig in the reconstructed Gladys City. 409-838-6581.

OCTOBER

Square Fair. Wharton's town square is the focus of an antique auto show, parade, dance, running races, etc. 409-532-1862.

Trinity Valley Exposition and Rodeo. Liberty gears up the third week of October with a variety of family activities, including a baby parade held annually since 1909. 409-336-5736.

Texas Prison Rodeo: The wildest rodeo behind bars brings visitors by the thousands to Huntsville on October Sundays. Expect a carnival and professional music entertainment also. 409-295-8113.

Renaissance Festival: The 16th century in Merrie Old England is recreated every weekend this month in the woods between Magnolia and Plantersville. Amid parades, jousting races, and games of skill, you'll chat with Robin Hood, assorted wenches, minstrels, comics, jugglers, knights and their elegant ladies, and other anachronistic characters. Dress to the theme and join in the fun. 713-356-2178; 409-894-2516.

Polk County Folklife Festival: Livingston spreads the fun around the courthouse square in downtown. There are street dances, trail rides, hot air balloon races, timber exhibits, food, crafts, etc. 409-327-4929.

Fall Fest: Canoe floats, field trips, and camping are part of the program on the grounds of the Big Thicket Museum in Saratoga. 409-274-5000.

Parada Del Rodeo: League City (south of Clear Lake) puts on a two-night rodeo followed by a dance in the pavilion at the Galveston County Park on T-3. There's also a trail ride and chili cook-off. 713-488-7676.

CavOilcade Celebration: Port Arthur's annual biggie, complete with street parade, old-timers breakfast, boat races, golf and tennis tournaments, Hungry Artists' show, antique automobiles, and a thieve's market. 409-985-7822.

Texas Rice Festival: The small town of Winnie (west of Beaumont on I-10) celebrates its prime crop with carnival, parades, art shows, rice-cooking contests, street and square dances, and professional entertainment. 409-296-2231.

Octoberfest: Washington-on-the-Brazos increases its population by several thousand on this two-day event. Expect a parade, street dance, entertainers, and loads of savory German food. 409-878-2112.

Strand Street Music Festival: Galveston seems to have more fun than almost any other town in the area. Details change on this offering, so call 409-740-2711 or 409-878-2112.

Epicurean Evening: How about sampling special dishes from the best restaurants in Galveston? This annual event is held in Moody Center on Seawall Boulevard. 409-763-4311.

Octoberfest: Round Top and Winedale combine efforts for this special celebration. Expect demonstrations of horseshoeing, muleskinning, fireplace cooking, soap making, etc., following a German heritage theme. 713-520-8057.

Scarecrow Festival: Chappell Hill's biggest event of the year, featuring a stew cook-off. 409-836-6382.

Antique Show: Bellville traditionally has one of the most extensive shows in the state on either the third or fourth weekend in October. The pavilion in the city park is the place. Also on the grounds are a farmer's market, pumpkin-decorating contest, folk art, quilting bee, rug weaving, pony rides, and country cooking. 409-865-5618; 409-865-5620.

Heritage Holiday: The Old West lives again in Old Town Spring, site of this annual ethnic clebration for northwest Harris County. 713-353-2317.

County and Regional Fairs: Try the Fort Bend County Fair at Rosenberg (713-342-5464) or the South Texas State Fair in Beaumont (409-838-6581). Other possibilities are the Brazoria County Fair (409-265-2505) and the Austin County Fair with its PCRA-sanctioned rodeo in Bellville (409-865-3407).

DECEMBER

Dickens's Evening on the Strand: Galveston's famous Strand becomes a four-block-long stage for Victorian Christmases past. Dress up in your best period duds and join the fun, a mix of characters from Dickens's many works, town criers, British Bobbies, carollers, etc. The Budweiser Clydesdales often are part of the 19th-century show. 713-488-5942; 409-765-7834.

Christmas Boat Lane Parade: Seabrook and Kemah join forces one evening to celebrate the season in their own unique way. 713-488-7676.

Glow of Christmas at Ashton Villa: One of Galveston's grandest homes is at its best during this annual event. 409-765-7921.

Christmas Open House at Winedale: All the old German Christmas traditions seem right at home here for this one night event. 409-278-3530.

Christmas Bird Count in Brazosport: This annual gathering for birders is planned between Christmas and New Year's and has resulted in the sighting of some 226 species in years past. Binoculars are essential. 409-265-2505.

Christmas Homes Tour in Wharton: Mansions of the past open their doors to the public. 409-532-1862.

Griffin House Christmas Candlelight Tour in Tomball: The traditional songs and wassail of Christmas on the second weekend of the month. 713-255-2148.

Montgomery Candlelight Tours: Lovely homes dressed for the season. 409-597-4155.

East Woods Press Books

American Bed & Breakfast
  Cook Book, The
Backcountry Cooking
Berkshire Trails for Walking & Ski Touring
Best Bed & Breakfast in the World, The
Blue Ridge Mountain Pleasures
California Bed & Breakfast
Campfire Chillers
Campfire Songs
Canoeing the Jersey Pine Barrens
Carolina Curiosities
Carolina Seashells
Carpentry: Some Tricks of the Trade from
  an Old-Style Carpenter
Catfish Cookbook, The
Charlotte: A Touch of Gold
Complete Guide to Backpacking
  in Canada
Creative Gift Wrapping
Day Trips From Baltimore
Day Trips From Cincinnati
Day Trips From Houston
Drafting: Tips and Tricks on Drawing and
  Designing House Plans
Exploring Nova Scotia
Fifty Years on the Fifty:
  The Orange Bowl Story
Fructose Cookbook, The
Grand Old Ladies
Grand Strand: An Uncommon Guide
  to Myrtle Beach, The
Healthy Trail Food Book, The
Hiking from Inn to Inn
Hiking Virginia's National Forests
Historic Country House Hotels
Hosteling USA, Third Edition
How to Afford Your Own Log Home
How to Play With Your Baby
Indiana: Off the Beaten Path
Interior Finish: More Tricks of the Trade
Just Folks: Visitin' with Carolina People
Kays Gary, Columnist
Maine Coast: A Nature Lover's
  Guide, The
Making Food Beautiful
Mid-Atlantic Guest House Book, The
New England Guest House Book, The
New England: Off the Beaten Path
Ohio: Off the Beaten Path
Parent Power!
Parks of the Pacific Coast
Race, Rock and Religion
River Reflections
Rocky Mountain National Park Hiking Trails
Saturday Notebook, The
Sea Islands of the South
Separation and Divorce in North Carolina
South Carolina Hiking Trails
Southern Guest House Book, The
Southern Rock: A Climber's Guide
  to the South

Sweets Without Guilt
Tar Heel Sights: Guide to North Carolina's
  Heritage
Tennessee Trails
Toys That Teach Your Child
Train Trips: Exploring America by Rail
Trout Fishing the Southern Appalachians
Vacationer's Guide to Orlando and
  Central Florida, A
Walks in the Catskills
Walks in the Great Smokies
Walks with Nature in Rocky Mountain
  National Park
Whitewater Rafting in Eastern America
Wildflower Folklore
Woman's Journey, A
You Can't Live on Radishes

Order from:

The East Woods Press
429 East Boulevard
Charlotte, NC 28203

You'll also enjoy these other guides...

The Best Bed & Breakfast in the World, 1984-1985, Sigourney Welles & Jill Darbey, $10.95 paper. More than 800 personally recommended establishments in Great Britain and Ireland with a special section on London and tear-out booking forms.

Train Trips: Exploring America by Rail, 1984-1985, William G. Scheller, $9.95 paper. Complete guide to U.S.'s Amtrak and Canada's Via Rail routes, with detailed visits to 52 major cities, including Houston.

The Southern Guest House Book, 1984-1985, Corinne Madden Ross, $7.95 paper. 107 lodgings in Alabama, Florida, Georgia, Louisiana, Mississippi, North Carolina, South Carolina, Tennessee, Virginia and the District of Columbia.

East Woods Press Pak-booksTM — Created with the outdoors in mind, these pocket-sized trail guides have sewn bindings, rounded outer corners and waterproofed and tear-resistant covers. From the Rocky Mountains to the East Coast, from hiking to campfire story-telling, they cover many regional outdoor activities. Send for a full description of these books in our free catalog.

Copies of these and other East Woods Press books are available from your bookseller or directly from The East Woods Press, 429 East Boulevard, Charlotte, N.C. 28203. (704) 334-0897. For orders **only**, call toll-free (800) 438-1242, ext. 102. In N.C. (800) 532-0476.

Please send me the following book(s)_____.
I am including $1.50 shipping and handling per book.
Enclosed is my check or use the Visa or MasterCard information below:

_____

Please send a complete catalog of East Woods Press books. ☐

Send to: _____

_____

_____

_____